BIRDS
of the Water, Sea, and Shore

Sandra D. Romashko

Illustrations By
Diana Manning

D1396935

𝕎𝕚𝕟𝕕𝕨𝕒𝕣𝕕 Publishing, Inc.

105 NE 25th St.   P.O. Box 371005   Miami, FL 33137

CONTENTS

INTRODUCTION

The birds selected for inclusion in this book are the water birds of North America, from Alaska to Baja California, Canada to Key West and including the Gulf of Mexico, Caribbean and West Indies.

At one time or another, we all see these birds—some magnificent, some noisy—but all part of the panorama of the seashore. Some are very common and easily identified; others are seldom seen. This book is intended to be an easy reference to identifying the birds you may encounter. The probability of seeing a particular bird in its range will be better if the particular *habitat* of the species is observed.

While some water birds have become familiar with humans and may be approached easily (such as pelicans, gulls which frequent fishing docks for handouts), most will flee from fast moving, noisy bird watchers. You will have the opportunity to observe more birds if you search alone or in small groups, walking quietly and slowly. Also, don't compete with the birds—wear dull colored clothing.

The water birds must not be molested nor their habitats and nests disturbed. Many are protected by law and cannot be taken, even with a collecting permit. A 35 mm camera with a 400 mm lens is the recommended equipment for "catching" the birds for your private enjoyment.

LOONS (Order: Gaviiformes; Family: Gaviidae)
Characterized by loud laughter-like calls, loons have specially adapted bodies which make them strong divers and swimmers, and therefore excellent at catching fish. With webbed feet set far back on the body, the loon is a clumsy waddling bird on land and thus comes ashore only to breed and nest. Their loud cries are heard primarily while breeding, but occasionally can be heard during other seasons. They feed on fish, crustaceans, and water plants. Sexes are alike.

Common Loon   *Gavia immer*   Length: 28-36 in. (71-91 cm.)
This most numerous species of loon breeds along lakes and rivers. Usually one pair of loons (often the same couple) return to the same lake each year to breed. The nest is built of matted grasses at the water's edge so the loon can come and go under water. The 1-3 olive green to dark brown eggs are spotted. The iridescent green-black head and neck are characteristic in summer. The bill is black and straight, the collar is streaked with white; underparts are white, and the black back is checkered with white. The young and winter adults have grey topsides and a white throat. *Range:* Northwest Alaska to Iceland, south to northeast California, northwest Montana, north Ohio and Newfoundland. Winters along coasts to northwest Mexico, the Gulf states and south Florida, and sometimes on the Great Lakes.

Red-throated Loon   *Gavia stellata*   Length: 24-27 in. (61-69 cm)
This smallest species of loon is common in its breeding range. The identifying neck patch is present only during the breeding season, but the species can always be identified by the slightly upturned lower bill. The nest is make of mud and wet plants at the edge of lakes or ponds; 1-3 eggs are olive green to dark brown. In summer this loon has a rust colored neck patch, white streaking on the back of the neck and a blackish brown back. The head is gray. The young and winter adults have a white throat and a spotted back. *Range:* Alaska to north Greenland, south to southwest British Columbia, north Manitoba, south Manitoba and Newfoundland. Winters on the Great Lakes and along both coasts to north Mexico and south Florida.

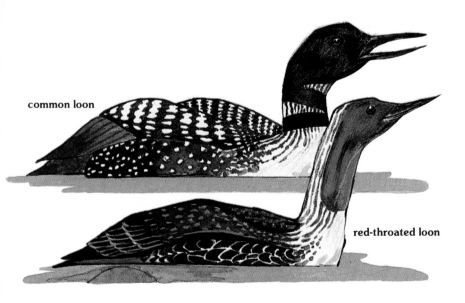

common loon

red-throated loon

GREBES (Order: Podicipediformes; Family: Podicipedidae)
Like the loons, grebes have their feet positioned far back on the body; the toes, however, are not webbed together but have overlapping broad flaps. They are good divers and swimmers but they must steer with their feet since they have almost no tail. They feed on small aquatic animals. Sexes are alike.

Least Grebe *Podiceps dominicus* Length: 8-10 in. (20-25 cm)
Within the U.S., our smallest grebe is found only in Texas. The nest is made of plant matter and mud and is anchored to emergent water plants; 4-6 white, pale green or bluish eggs are incubated by by both sexes. It has a short neck and a short straight bill. The crown, chin and back are black; the eye is orange; wing patch and undersides are white. Winter color variation includes white chin, brownish cap and golden eye. *Range:* Baja California to south Texas, south to Argentina; West Indies.

Western Grebe *Aechmophorus occidentalis* Length: 22-29 in. (56-74 cm)
Characterized by a long straight neck, this species is also sometimes called swan grebe. Abundant within their range, these are the largest North American grebes. Nests are built out of plants in large colonies, sometimes in shallow water or on submerged plants; 3-4 eggs are pale blue-green or buff. The long, pointed bill is yellow; upper parts are blackish; face, throat, wing patch and underparts are white. *Range:* From Canada south to central California, north North Dakota, locally from southwest Colorado to southwest Minnesota. Winters along Pacific coast to west Mexico; rare visitor to Great Lakes and Atlantic and Gulf coasts.

Red-necked Grebe *Podiceps grisegena* Length: 18-22 in. (46-56 cm)
Also known as Holboell's grebe, this species is distinguished from the other grebes by the heavy bill and contrast in color between the throat and neck at all times of the year. They are uncommon and found inland on secluded northern lakes in summer. A nest of marsh plants anchored to upright plants floats on water; 3-6 eggs are blue white. The bill is yellowish; the black, tufted crown is marked with green. Cheeks, underparts, wing patches and linings are white; the back is dark gray and the throat is reddish. The crown is brown and the throat and face crescent are white in winter. *Range:* From northwest Alaska to northwest Ontario, south to north Washington and south Minnesota, and occasionally east to New Hampshire. Winters along coasts to south California and central Florida.

Horned Grebe *Podiceps auritus* Length: 12-15 in. (30-38 cm)
In summer both male and female have a reddish-yellow plume on each side of the head for which they are named. A very common grebe, it is found in lakes and ponds during breeding season, and winters in salt water along the coast and into the Great Lakes. The nest is a mass of plants anchored to reeds or bushes; 4-5 eggs are blue white to olive white. The bill is thin and dark; crown and cheeks are black; reddish-yellow 'horns'. The back is dark; throat, sides, breast and rump are reddish brown; belly and wing patch are white. In winter the underparts and cheeks are white. *Range:* From west Alaska to north New York and Nova Scotia, south to east Idaho and Wisconsin. Winters along coasts to southern California, to south Florida and along Gulf coast.

Eared Grebe *Podiceps caspicus* Length: 12-14 in. (30-36 cm)
These small grebes are named for the bright tuft of feathers behind each eye. These birds congregate in colonies during the breeding season and build their nests simultaneously within a few feet of each other. The poorly constructed floating nest is made of rushes, cattails; 3-4 eggs are dull blue white or green white. They are found in shallow lakes and sloughs during summer. Tawny 'ears' adorn the crested black head; bill is slightly upturned. Back is dark; neck and breast are black; sides brownish; wing patch and belly are white. In winter, the breast, cheeks and neck are white. *Range:* British Columbia to west Minnesota, south to Baja California, central Arizona and south Texas. Winters south to Columbia.

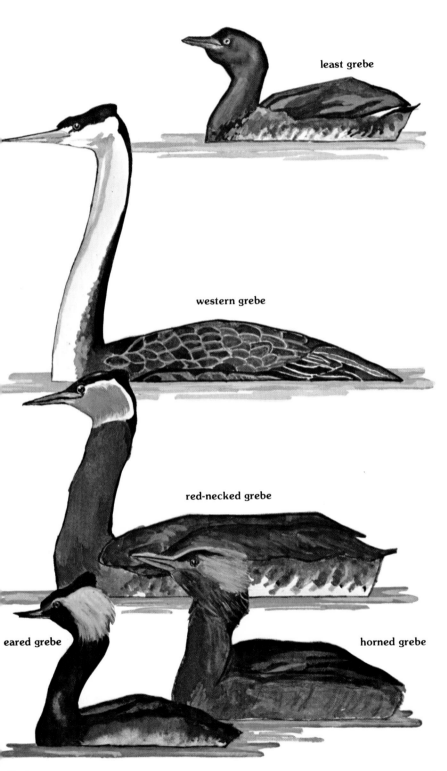

least grebe

western grebe

red-necked grebe

eared grebe

horned grebe

Grebes

ALBATROSSES   (Order: Procellariiformes; Family: Diomedeidae)
All members of this order are characterized by the cylindrical nasal tubes found on the top of the beak—"tubenoses." Albatrosses are the largest members of the order, and most species are found in the southern hemisphere. They have long, narrow wings and a heavy hooked beak. These seabirds come to land only to breed where they nest in colonies and lay a single egg. They feed on fish, squid and other marine life found while skimming the waters surface. They are commonly called "gooney" birds. Sexes are similar.

Laysan Albatross   *Diomedea immutabilis*   Length: 30 in. (76 cm)
This gray and white albatross is similar in appearance to an overgrown seagull. They have an extremely good homing ability, able to find their way back to their nesting grounds from more than 4000 miles away. The egg is white to buff, with or without reddish-brown spotted ends. It has a white neck, head, rump, underparts and wing linings. Back, wings and tail are blackish gray; feet are pink. *Range:* From Islands of Hawaii it roams over open sea to Japan and coast of North America from Aleutians to Baja California.

Black-footed Albatross   *Diomedea nigripes*   Length: 28 in. (71 cm)
This is the only albatross found off North America coasts that is dark all over. Often it can be found resting on the water. Egg is white, spotted with red-brown. The body is large and sooty colored; belly is gray, feet are black, face is whitish. Young are dark brown. *Range:* From the Islands of Hawaii it roams over open sea to east Asia coast and coast of North America from Aleutians to south Baja California.

FULMARS and **SHEARWATERS**   (Order: Procellariiformes; Family: Procellariidae)
These tubenoses are considerably smaller than the albatrosses, but have the same nesting, breeding and feeding habits. The bill has a pronounced tooth at the end. Sexes are similar.

Northern Fulmar   *Fulmarus glacialis*   Length: 17-20 in. (43-51 cm)
The fulmar has a light and dark color phase. In the lighter phase it resembles the herring gull, but can be distinguished by its shorter beak, heavy head and neck and tubular nose. When threatened, the fulmar sprays a foul smelling stomach oil at intruders. It nests in rocky cliffs and is usually found far out at sea. The egg is white, sometimes with red spots. The stubby bill is yellow; head and underparts are white. In light phase, back and wings are grayish white; in dark phase, they are smoky gray. *Range:* Arctic waters of Alaska, Canada to Greenland. Winters to waters off Baja California and New England.

Audubon's Shearwater   *Puffinus lherminieri*   Length: 11-12 in. (28-30 cm)
This small warm water species is rather common and breeds in the Bahamas. Egg is white. It has a thin dark bill, dark crown and back and whitish underparts. *Range:* Atlantic waters from Bermuda to the West Indies; frequent off Florida coast and occasionally roams to Maine coast.

Greater Shearwater   *Puffinus gravis*   Length: 18-20 in. (46-51 cm)
A large and fairly common tubenose, the greater shearwater is readily identified by the sharp contrast between the top of the head and throat and the white marking on the tail. During the breeding season, the entire population congregates on three small islands in the Tristan da Cunha group. Egg is white. They have a thin dark bill, black crown, gray-brown back, white band on tail and white underparts. *Range:* Most of Atlantic Ocean.

Sooty Shearwater   *Puffinus griseus*   Length: 16-18 in. (41-46 cm)
This large bird is common in the fall off the west coast of North America, uncommon off the east coast. Egg is white. The body and bill are dark gray-brown, wing linings are pale gray. *Range:* Roams over most of the Pacific, Atlantic, and South Indian Oceans.

Laysan albatross

black-footed albatross

Audubon's shearwater

northern fulmar

ater shearwater

sooty shearwater

7

STORM PETRELS (Order: Procellariiformes, Family: Hydrobatidae)
These small open water birds have tubular nostrils, a sturdy hooked beak, and fairly long legs. They feed on small fish, shrimp and plankton. Storm petrels can be found in flocks or singly; they lay only one egg. Sexes are alike.

Fork-tailed Petrel *Oceanodroma furcata* Length: 8-9 in. (20-23 cm)
The most brigtly colored of the storm petrels, the fork-tail is common in its breeding range in the northern Pacific. They nest on sea islands in a burrow or rock crevice, and tend to glide more than other petrels. The single white egg has a ring of dark spots around the larger end. The bird's undersides are whitish, top parts are light gray; they have a dark eye patch and wing lining and a forked tail. *Range:* Aleutian Islands south to northern California; wanders to southern California and Japan.

Black Petrel *Oceanodroma melania* Length: 9 in. (23 cm)
This largest and most common all-dark petrel nests in burrows or rock crannies. It eats spiny lobster larvae, plankton, small fishes; it follows ships at sea. This petrel has long legs and a forked tail. The body is blackish brown with a pale bar on top of each wing. *Range:* Islands off Baja California, wanders to coast of central California. Winters south to waters off Peru.

Leach's Petrel *Oceanodroma leucorhoa* Length: 7.5-9 in. (19-23 cm)
This uncommon bird is similar to Wilson's petrel in appearance, but can be distinguished by the forked tail. They also eat small squids in addition to fishes, crustaceans, and refuse from ships—but they do not follow them. They nest in 1-3 foot deep tunnels. The body is blackish brown, feet are dark, rump is white, and the tail is forked. *Range:* Wide ranging in northern hemisphere. Aleutian Islands, southeast to Baja California; wanders to Hawaii and Galapagos Islands. Massachusetts to Labrador, wandering southward to the equator.

Wilson's Petrel *Oceanites oceanicus* Length: 7 in. (18 cm)
This species is common during summer months off the Atlantic coast. It can be identified by the square tail and yellow webs between the toes. It eats plankton, small fishes, squid and unregimented flocks often follow ships and fishing boats at sea to pick up scraps. Nests in burrows or crevices under rocks; single white egg has a ring of fine dark dots around the larger end. The bird is gray brown, has a white rump and whitish wing patch and a square tail. *Range:* Breeds in antarctic and islands off southern South America; widely spread northward to Labrador and California.

fork-tailed petrel

black petrel

Leach's petrel

Wilson's petrel

TROPICBIRDS   (Order: Pelecaniformes, Family: Phaethontidae)

White-tailed Tropicbird   *Phaethon lepturus*   Length: 32 in. (81 cm)
As adults, these fish-eating birds have a 16-19 in. (41-48 cm) long tail (included in the overall length given above). Can be seen occasionally off the southeast coast of U.S. after storms. They feed on small fishes, squids, and crabs caught by diving from high above the water. They nest on bare rock on remote islands and lay a single pinkish, speckled egg each season. The four toes have webbing between them. The head, body and tail streamers are white; black eye stripe and band on the wing; orange bill. Immature birds have a barred back and lack the long tail streamers. Sexes are alike. *Range:* Bermuda, Bahamas, the Caribbean, tropical islands in Atlantic, Pacific and Indian Oceans; U.S. coast from North Carolina to Florida.

PELICANS   (Order: Pelecaniformes, Family: Pelecanidae)
These are the largest birds of the order. They are powerful flyers, feed on fish and have webbed feet with webbing between all four toes. They are easily identified by the large pouch under the long bill. The pouch is used as a scoop to catch fish when the pelican dives; the water is drained between the mandibles. Sexes are alike.

Brown Pelican   *Pelecanus occidentalis*   Length: 41-54 in. (104-137 cm)
The brown pelican is locally common on the coasts where it nests in colonies on the ground or in trees. They lay 3-5 eggs. They dive into the water from heights of 30 feet. Accustomed to hand outs, they will beg for fish scraps on fishing docks. Adults have a gray-brown body and a light colored head and, in summer, a reddish brown back of the neck. Immature bird is dull brown overall, with light undersides. *Range:* East coast of U.S. from North Carolina to British Guiana, including the Gulf of Mexico, Cuba, Bahamas, West Indies. On the west coast from southern British Columbia south to Chile. Isolated population on the Galapagos Islands.

White Pelican   *Pelecanus erythrorhynchos*   Length: 54-70 in. (137-178 cm)
This bird has a huge wingspan which may reach 9.5 feet. They do not dive but swim in shallow water scooping up the fish in the pouch. They can be found in both fresh and salt water within their range. Adults are white overall except for black on the tip and trailing edges of the wings. The huge bill is yellowish but is orange with a "knob" on the upper bill during breeding season. Immature birds have a grayish bill and gray tuft on the top of the head. *Range:* British Columbia to southwest Ontario, south to southeast California and northwest Wyoming; southeast Texas. Winters to Guatemala and Florida.

FRIGATEBIRDS   (Order: Pelecaniformes, Family: Fregatidae)

Magnificent Frigatebird   *Fregata magnificens*   Length: 38-41 in. (96-104 cm)
This bird is common in the Florida Keys during the summer; can be seen occasionally in its other locales during storms. They nest on rock promontories or open treetops and lay one egg which is incubated by both parents taking turns. It feeds by taking small fish or other marine scraps from the surface of the water, but does not sit on the water. Adults are black with a long hooked bill and a long forked tail. Males have an orange throat pouch which turns red during breeding. The red pouch is inflated during courtship which he may keep distended until the egg is hatched. Females have white breasts. Immature birds have white head, neck and breast. *Range:* Islands of Pacific from Baja California to Ecuador and in the Atlantic from the Bahamas to Brazil and the Cape Verdes Islands. Seen off northern California and from Texas to Florida.

Tropicbird, Pelicans, Frigatebird

white-tailed tropicbird

brown pelican

white pelican

magnificent frigatebird

Tropicbird, Pelicans, Frigatebird

BOOBIES AND GANNETS (Order: Pelecaniformes, Family: Sulidae)
These high-diving seabirds, like the other members of order Pelecaniformes, have all four toes webbed. They dive for fish from great heights over the water and then chase the prey under the surface. Sexes are alike.

Brown Booby *Sula leucogaster* Length: 28-30 in. (71-76 cm)
Flying fishes and halfbeaks are the staple of the brown booby's diet, but it will eat other fishes as well. They lay one or two bluish eggs which are incubated in turn by both parents. This bird has dark brown upper body parts with a white belly which is clearly defined against the dark breast. Feet and bill are yellow. Immature bird is dark above and lacks the defined contrast below. *Range:* Islands from Bahamas to Brazil, Gulf coast and east coast of Florida; tropical islands in Pacific, and rarely off the coast of southeast California.

Masked Booby (Blue-faced Booby) *Sula dactylatra* Length: 27 in. (69 cm)
The blue-faced booby feeds throughout the day on flying fishes and small squids. The nest is built on islands in colonies or scattered groups; 1-2 eggs are chalky white. The body and head are white and the skin on the face near the bill is slate colored. The tail and entire rear edge of the wing are black. Immature bird is dusky and has a whitish patch on upper back and rump. One or two chalky bluish eggs are tended by both parents. *Range:* Tropical oceans; east coast from South Carolina to Florida (especially Dry Tortugas) and Texas; islands off west coast of Mexico.

Gannet *Morus bassanus* Length: 35-40 in. (89-102 cm)
These spectacular divers may be seen dropping to 50 feet below the surface in dives with 10 foot high sprays. They prey on schooling fishes such as herring and menhadden. Both sexes incubate the single chalky blue egg. The head is creamy, body is white with black wing tips. Both tail and bill are sharply pointed. Immature bird is dusky. *Range:* North Atlantic from Gulf of St. Lawrence to Iceland and the British Isles; winters south to Gulf of Mexico and east coast of Florida.

CORMORANT (Order: Pelecaniformes; Family: Phalacrocoracidae) and
ANHINGA (Order: Pelecaniformes; Family: Anhingidae)
These birds are fish eaters that dive from the surface and swim underwater in pursuit of their prey. As the other members of the order, the feet are webbed between all four toes. They are often seen perched on rocks, pilings, etc. with the wings expanded to dry.

Double-crested Cormorant *Phalacrocorax auritus* Length: 30-36 in. (76-91 cm)
This is the most common cormorant and it can be easily recognized by its perching stance—body erect and neck in an S-shape. They swim low in the water with the erect head showing and bill tilted upward. Sexes are similar. It catches mainly fishes of no commercial value; salamanders; some crustaceans, reptiles, mollusks and worms. The nest is built by both parents, in colonies, and may be reused; 2-7 eggs are pale blue, usually stained. The bill is hooked and they have an orange throat pouch; upper back is bronze; head, neck and lower back are black with greenish cast. Both male and female have crests on either side of the head—for which they are named—but these disappear soon after nesting begins. Immature birds are brownish with whitish breast and dark belly. *Range:* Most of North America, south to southern Mexico, Florida and West Indies. Winters to Central America.

Anhinga *Anhinga anhinga* Length: 34 in. (86 cm)
This bird does not dive for prey; rather it swims with the body submerged and only head and long, slender neck showing above the water. He swims with the head back and neck in an S-shape, prowling alertly. When prey is spotted the beak darts forward, and the victim is skewered by the long pointy bill. It will eat fish, aquatic insects, crayfish, frogs, water snakes, small alligators and terrapins. The anhinga's nest is found along with nests of herons and egrets. The nest is built of sticks and lined with moss and green cypress foliage; 1-5 eggs are chalky blue. The neck is long and slender, bill is long and pointed; body is black with greenish cast; wing patches are silver, and tail is long. Female has buffy neck and breast; immature birds are brownish. *Range:* Southeastern United States from southern Oklahoma and eastern Texas to eastern North Carolina, south to Argentina.

brown booby

masked booby

gannet

double-crested cormorant

anhinga

WATERFOWL   (Order: Anseriformes; Family: Anatidae)

Geese, swans and ducks make up the informal grouping of birds we commonly call waterfowl. This family is broken down into seven subfamilies: one for geese, one for swans, and five for ducks. Waterfowl are aquatic, have a flattened bill with small tooth-like serations, called lamellae, used for straining. They have four toes on each foot, the first three of which are webbed; their legs are short, wide-set and powerful. The body of these birds is covered with a heavy coat of down which is covered by thick feathers; when these flight feathers are molted (all at once), the bird is unable to fly until new feathers appear. They have well insulated, buoyant bodies and the young are covered with down and can walk and swim shortly after being hatched.

GEESE   (Subfamily: Anserinae)

Geese have longer necks than ducks, and are larger and heavier. As an adaptation to grazing, the legs are placed farther forward on the body than the legs of swans and ducks. The bill is broad and has a rounded tip; geese feed on grass, grains and some marine vegetation. They molt once a year and lay 3-8 eggs. Sexes are alike.

White-fronted goose   *Anser albifrons*   Length: 26-34 in. (66-86 cm)
The white-fronted goose has a loud laugh-like call which is the basis for another common name, "laughing goose". The nest is constructed of grass and normally holds 5-6 buff colored eggs. The goslings are olive colored. The white-fronted goose has a white muzzle, a pink bill which changes to blue at the base, and gray-brown underparts. The off-white breast and belly are marked with speckles of black. The feet are yellow. The young bird lacks the white face mark and the whitish belly, and resembles the blue goose except that the white-fronted goose has yellow feet instead of dark feet. *Range:* Arctic tundra; winters to Mexico, Gulf states.

Blue Goose   *Chen caerulescens*   Length: 23-38 in. (58-97 cm)
This is the blue phase of the snow goose. The nests, which contain 3-5 white eggs, are made of moss and grass and are lined with down. Their primary food is marsh plants. The neck and head are white, but the head is often stained with rust. The body is gray-brown, wings have blue-gray and black markings. The immature bird has a gray head and neck. *Range:* Arctic; migrates to Gulf of Mexico.

Canada Goose   *Branta canadensis*   Length: 22-43 in. (56-109 cm)
This is the most widely distributed goose species and consists of 11 races, or subspecies, ranging in size from 4-18 lbs. These geese feed on waste grain, shoots of new crops, and sometimes roots of aquatic plants. They lay 5-6 cream colored eggs; goslings are yellow green. The Canada goose has a black head and neck, white "cheeks" and "chin", white tail coverts and belly. Feet are black, back is gray-brown to dark brown, breast is gray to brown. *Range:* Widespread; Alaska, Canada, northern U.S.; winters to Mexico.

Snow Goose   *Chen caerulescens*   Length: 23-38 in. (58-97 cm)
This is a coastal species that feeds on salt marsh grasses. They lay 4-8 white eggs. The body is white, wings have black tips, bill and feet are pink, and the head is often rusty. The young are light gray and have a dark bill. *Range:* Arctic coasts; winters to central Mexico and western Florida, and along the Atlantic coast from New Jersey to North Carolina.

SWANS   (Subfamily: Cygninae)

Whistling Swan   *Olor columbianus*   Length: 47-58 in. (119-147 cm)
This is our most common swan. They dip the long neck and head into water to feed on bottom vegetation; they also graze on shore grasses. Sexes are similar. The nest is a mound of dried grasses usually on small islands in tundra pools; the 4-5 eggs are dull white. The body is white, the bill is black with a yellow spot at the base. Young birds are grayish with pinkish bills. *Range:* Alaska to Baffin Island; winters to northern Baja California and North Carolina, sometimes to Florida and the Gulf coast.

white-fronted goose

Canada goose

blue goose

whistling swan

snow goose

SURFACE-FEEDING DUCKS (Subfamily: Anatinae)
This group of ducks feeds on weeds from fresh and brackish waters, occasionally on grain from fields. They are characterized by having a bright speculum on the rear of each wing. When compared to diving ducks, these ducks have smaller feet and the hind toes do not have a wide flap or lobe. The males are usually more brightly colored than the females, except in summer after the breeding season when molting occurs and the male resembles the female.

Mallard *Anas platyrhynchos* Length: 20-28 in. (51-71 cm)
The mallard is the most abundant waterfowl in North America, and is the ancestor of domesticated types which are raised commercially. They nest in reeds on dry ground near water; 8-12 buff eggs hatch into yellow and sepia ducklings. Both male and female have violet speculums bordered with black and white, and have white wing linings. The male has a green head, white collar and white outer tail feathers. The back is brown, rump is black, breast is chestnut, and the belly is gray. The female is mottled brown and has paler underparts. *Range:* Northwest Alaska to southern Ontario, south to Baja California, Texas, Illinois and Virginia; winters to central Mexico.

American Widgeon *Anas americana* Length: 16-20 in. (41-51 cm)
These ducks relish roots of water celery and other deep aquatic plants, but since they do not dive they often steal these foods from diving ducks. They build a nest of leaves on weed covered islets or on a grassland away from water and lay 9-11 creamy-white eggs. Both sexes have a gray neck, small blue bill, white patch on forewing, green and black speculum, whitish belly. Males have a white crown and flank patch, iridescent green head patch, pinky-brown body. Female has a gray head and brown body. *Range:* Western Alaska to Manitoba, south to northern California, northern Arizona, Nebraska, western Pennsylvania; winters to Central America and the West Indies.

Black Duck *Anas rubripes* Length: 21-25 in. (53-64 cm)
The black duck is more common in the eastern part of the United States. They winter in coastal marshes and wooded swamps; many live in the Mississippi and Great Lake drainages. They feed on mollusks in open water during the day, and in salt marshes during twilight hours. The nest containing 6-12 greenish-tan eggs is hidden in grass or under brush. The body is dark mottled brown, speculum is violet and bordered in black, wing lining white, feet are reddish brown. Sexes are similar but breast feathers of male are marked with a rounded "U" pattern; female's are marked with a "V". *Range:* Northern Manitoba to Newfoundland, south to North Dakota and North Carolina; winters to southeast Texas and Florida.

Mottled Duck *Anas fulvigula* Length: 20 in. (51 cm)
The mottled duck eats mollusks, insects, and fish in addition to its vegetable diet of aquatic plants and seeds. The nest, holding 8-11 greenish eggs, is on high ground near salt or brackish water. Both sexes are similar, resembling the female mallard. Mottled ducks have a yellow or orange bill, brownish crown with buff face and throat. Body is mottled brown, speculum is purple with black border, wing lining is white. *Range:* Coasts of Texas, Louisiana, Florida; Mexico and South America.

Pintail *Anas acuta* Length: 20-30 in. (51-76 cm)
These ducks have longer necks than most surface-feeding ducks which allow them to feed deeper in the water without upending. The long tail of the male is characteristic of the species. They feed on water plants and seeds, some mollusks, and insects. Their nest is lined with straw and down and holds 6-10 greenish or tan eggs. Both sexes have a greenish-brown speculum with a white border on one edge. The male has a brown head, white throat, white stripes on neck and breast, gray back, long thin tail. The female is mottled brown and has a short pointed tail. *Range:* Arctic regions of northern hemisphere south to southern California, northwest Pennsylvania; winters south to Central America.

mallard

American widgeon

black duck

mottled duck

pintail

Ducks

Blue-winged Teal *Anas discors* Length: 14-16.5 in. (36-42 cm)
These ducks are concentrated in the prairie country of the United States and Canada. They prefer to feed in very shallow water where they eat tender parts of aquatic plants, seeds, water insects and mollusks. The nest is made of grass and down and holds 8-10 cream-colored eggs. Both sexes have a blue patch on the forewing and a green speculum with one white edge. The male has a slate gray head, white face crescent, brownish back, spotted light-brown undersides and a white patch on each flank. The female is mottled brown with a whitish underside. *Range:* British Columbia and Saskatchewan to Nova Scotia, south to California and North Carolina; winters south to Brazil.

Green-winged Teal *Anas carolinensis* Length: 12.5-15.5 in. (32-39 cm)
This very handsome bird is the smallest of all our waterfowl. It is considered by some to be a subspecies of the European green-winged teal, *Anas crecca crecca,* which is distributed world-wide in the northern hemisphere. They eat seeds of bulrush, pondweed, sedge, and panic grass; animal food includes insects and mollusks. The nest is placed in a hollow in high grass, usually near water; 10-12 whitish eggs are laid. The greenwing has a green and black speculum with a buff border, whitish belly. The male has a chestnut head with a slight crest and a green patch; back is gray brown and the front of the wing is marked with a white bar. The female has brownish back and sides. *Range:* Alaska to Newfoundland, south to California, New Mexico, Minnesota, Ohio and Massachusetts; winters south to Central America and the West Indies.

Wood Duck *Aix sponsa* Length: 17-20 in. (43-51 cm)
The female wood duck nests in the same spot year after year or in an area where she was hatched. Hollows in trees as high as 50 feet above ground are used as nests for the 10-15 white eggs. In water, wood ducks feed on insects and duckweed. On land they eat acorns. All wood ducks are crested and have a white throat and belly. The male has a white-striped face, and the head and back are iridescent green, bronze, and purple. The wood duck female is more colorful than females of other species of ducks. She has a gray-brown face, tan flanks, and a white patch around the eye. *Range:* British Columbia to Montana and central California, and Manitoba to Nova Scotia south to Texas and Cuba; winters to central Mexico.

Cinnamon Teal *Anas cyanoptera* Length: 14.5-17 in. (37-43 cm)
The cinnamon teal is closely related and similar in behavior to the blue-winged teal. Females of the two species are almost identical in appearance, except the bill on the cinnamon teal is longer. A grass nest is built in reeds and will hold 6-12 off-white eggs. They feed on bulrush, pondweed, saltgrass, sedge, insects and mollusks. Both sexes have a blue patch on each forewing, a green speculum with a white edge, and whitish wing lining. The male is cinnamon-red on the chest and head; the female is mottled brown. *Range:* British Columbia to Saskatchewan, south to central Mexico; winters to Panama and Columbia.

Shoveler *Anas clypeata* Length: 17-20 in. (43-51 cm)
The large spoon-shaped bill is equipped with comb-like teeth which strain larvae and small crustaceans from the mud the "spoonbill" feeds in. Nests are built in tall grasses near a pond or slough, and the 6-12 eggs are buff or gray colored. Male and female have a huge bill, blue wing patch, green speculum with a white border, orange legs, and white wing lining. The male has a blackish-green head and rump, white chest, upper back and flank patch; belly and sides are chestnut. The female is mottled brown. *Range:* Alaska to Hudson Bay, south to California, New Mexico, Nebraska, Alabama and Delaware; winters to Hawaii, Central America, and the West Indies.

Ducks

blue-winged teal

green-winged teal

wood duck

cinnamon teal

shoveler

Ducks

DIVING DUCKS (Subfamily: Aythyinae)
Diving ducks can be distinguished from surface-feeding ducks by their legs and feet. The legs on diving ducks are located farther back and are farther apart than the dabblers'; the feet are larger and have large lobes on the hind toes. Much of their lives are spent at sea where they dive for food.

Canvasback *Aythya valisineria* Length: 19.5-24 in. (50-61 cm)
Cans, as they are called, resemble the redhead but are larger, have a long neck, and their backs are very white. Normal diet is primarily wild celery with some snails and crustaceans. The nest is a platform of intertwined plants over shallow water and holds 7-9 greenish-gray eggs. Canvasbacks are characterized by their long sloping head and long dark bill. The male has a brownish-red head and neck, black breast, white body. The female is brown on the head, neck and breast, and has a grayish body. *Range:* Alaska to Manitoba, south to California, Utah, and Minnesota; winters south to Mexico.

Redhead *Aythya americana* Length 18-22 in. (46-56 cm)
Redheads are often found in the company of canvasbacks and scaups. They eat leaves and stems of aquatic plants, dive for other vegetation, and also feed in shallows on water insects and small shellfish. Nests are made of matted grasses, and 10-15 creamy eggs are laid. They have a blue bill with black tip and whitish wing patch. The male has a brownish-red head and neck, a black rump, chest and tail; the back is gray and undersides are white. The female is brown and has a light face patch near the bill. *Range:* Western Canada to Minnesota, south to California, Wisconsin, and Pennsylvania; winters to Mexico and the West Indies.

Ring-necked Duck *Aythya collaris* Length: 15-18 in. (38-46 cm)
These birds are primarily vegetarians but they also eat insects and snails. The grassy nest is built over water or at the edge of a pond and normally contains 8-12 olive-tan eggs. Both sexes have a peaked crown, a bill with two whitish rings, and a light-gray speculum. The male has a black head, chest and back, chestnut neck ring, and white wedge on the sides. The wings, belly and tail are dark. The female has white eye rings; back is brown, undersides are white. *Range:* Canada and northern United States; winters to Panama and West Indies.

Greater Scaup *Aythya marila* Length: 16-20 in. (41-51 cm)
These birds are good divers and can remain under water for a long time. They eat shellfish and wild celery and grasses near shore. They breed in the arctic and lay 7-10 olive-tan eggs in a nest built of matted plants. They have a blue bill and long white stripe on the wing. The male has a black head and neck with a greenish cast, white back and sides, and a black chest and tail. The female is brown with a white face and belly. *Range:* Alaska and northern Canada; winters on Pacific coast from southern Alaska to California, and along the coast of the middle Atlantic and Gulf states.

Lesser Scaup *Aythya affinis* Length: 15-18 in. (38-46 cm)
The greater and lesser scaups are very similar in size and appearance. The lesser is only slightly smaller and if viewed in sunlight, generally has a purple tone to the head while the greater has a green cast. The down-lined nest is built on the ground and holds 9-12 olive-tan eggs. They feed on pondweed, snails and water insects. They have a blue bill, white breast, white stripe on the wing. The male has a black head and neck with a purple gloss; back is whitish, sides are gray, tail and chest are black. The female is brown and has a white face and belly. *Range:* Alaska and western Canada; winters south to northern South America, West Indies.

Ducks

canvasback

redhead

ring-necked duck

greater scaup

lesser scaup

Ducks

Common Goldeneye *Bucephala clangula* Length: 16-20 in. (41-51 cm)
The American goldeneye, as this species is also known, is commonly found in lakes and rivers in wooded areas. Their diet consists of crustaceans, insects and mollusks. These ducks lay 8-12 greenish eggs in a tree cavity or rotting stump near water; the eggs are covered with down. Both sexes have white wing patches. The male has a green-black head, high crown, white face patch and undersides, and a black back. The female has a brown head, white collar, and gray body. *Range:* Alaska to Quebec and Newfoundland, south to British Columbia and Maine; winters from Alaska, Nebraska, Minnesota, and Newfoundland to California and the Gulf coast.

Barrow's Goldeneye *Bucephala islandica* Length: 16.5-20 in. (42-51 cm)
Barrow's goldeneyes feed in fresh water on pondweed, water insects, crayfish, and other crustaceans. Nests are built in cavities of decaying trees near water or in some other shelter; 6-15 pale green eggs are laid. Male and female have white wing patches. The male has a purple-black head with a white face crescent—which distinguishes it from the common goldeneye—, white underparts, and a black body. The female has a brown head and white collar, and gray body. In spring and early summer the female can be distinguished from the common goldeneye by her completely yellow bill—not black with a yellow tip as is the common's. *Range:* Alaska and northwest Canada south to California and Colorado, and Labrador and Greenland; winters along Pacific coast to California and along the Atlantic coast to New York.

Bufflehead *Bucephala albeola* Length: 13-15.5 in. (33-39 cm)
Buffleheads are the smallest of the diving ducks. Their small size along with the white patch on their relatively large head identify both male and female. Their diet consists of fish, shrimp and mussels. They build their nests in trees in old large wookpecker holes where they lay 10-12 ivory eggs. Buffleheads have white wing patches and a large head relative to their small size. The male has a black iridescent head with a large white crown, a black back and white undersides. The female is gray and has a pale breast and white cheeks. *Range:* Alaska to Ontario, south to British Columbia and Montana, mountains of Oregon and California; winters from Alaska, Great Lakes, New Brunswick, south to Mexico.

STIFF-TAILED DUCKS (Subfamily: Oxyurinae)
These are small stubby ducks that have a short thick neck. While swimming they often hold the spiky tail up at an angle. They have difficulty moving about on land.

Ruddy Duck *Oxyura jamaicensis* Length: 14.5-16 in. (37-41 cm)
The ruddy duck is common in summer on lakes and ponds and during winter on estuaries, lakes, and rivers. They eat pondweed seeds and stems and dive for wild celery and mollusks. The nest is a woven platform of vegetation attached to vertical stems as support several inches above shallow water; 6-10 very large white eggs are laid. Ruddy ducks are small, have white cheeks, and a stiff tail. The male is capable of holding his tail erect and has two complete plumages. He is rust-red with a black crown, and blue bill most of the year, but he is gray in winter. The female is gray with a dark stripe on each cheek. *Range:* Canada south to northern South America; winters to Costa Rica and the Bahamas.

Masked Duck *Oxyura dominica* Length: 20 in. (51 cm)
This tropical species is closely related to the ruddy duck. It nests in trees and is found primarily around fresh water. Large white wing patches distinguish it from the ruddy duck. Male has black face; female has dark face lines. *Range:* Southeastern United States, Mexico, West Indies.

common goldeneye

Barrow's goldeneye

bufflehead

ruddy duck

masked duck

Ducks

SEA DUCKS (Subfamily: Aythyinae)
These birds are usually seen along coastlines, rarely inland. They are large, heavy, have short necks, and are diving ducks. Food for most sea ducks is mollusks.

Surf Scoter *Melanitta perspicillata* Length: 17-21 in. (43-53 cm)
This is the most widely distributed scoter. They dive and feed on shellfish and the surf scoter earned its name from its habit of feeding on the breaking surf. The nest is built in bushes near a lake or pond and holds 5-9 buff eggs. The surf scoter is smaller than the white-winged scoter, has a thick neck, reddish feet. The male has white patches on the forehead and nape, and red and black patches on a heavy white bill. The brown female has two prominent white spots on each side of the face. *Range:* Alaska and northern Canada; winters to southern Atlantic and Pacific coasts.

White-winged Scoter *Melanitta deglandi* 19-23.5 in. (48-60 cm)
This largest scoter eats insects, pondweed, and dives to search for mussels, oysters and scallops. The nest is hidden under bushes near a pond or lake and contains 9-14 pinky-tan eggs. This is a large bird which has a thick neck, swollen bill, white wing patch, and reddish feet. The male is dark and has a white eye patch and orange bill with a black protuberance at the base. The female is dusky brown and has two light patches on the side of the face. *Range:* Alaska and northern Canada; winters to southern U.S. Atlantic and Gulf coasts and Pacific coasts of U.S. and Baja California.

Oldsquaw *Clangula hyemalis* 15-22 in. (38-56 cm)
These noisy and very hardy winter ducks were given their name by fur traders and Indians because of their constant chatter. They are extremely good divers and can go to depths of 180-200 feet to find mollusks and crustaceans. They lay 5-7 olive-buff eggs in a depression in grass. The male is brownish-black with white eye patches, white flanks and belly; sharply-pointed tail is long. In winter, he has a white head, neck and shoulders, a dark face patch, back and breast. The female has a dark crown, face patch and back; the whitish head and underparts are paler in winter. *Range:* Arctic species which winters on both United States coasts.

Common Eider *Somateria mollissima* Length: 23-27 in. (58-69 cm)
The common eider is a very important commercial duck since the gray eiderdown from the breast is used as insulation for cold weather gear and fine bedding. The nests are in crevices or pits and are down lined and hold 4-6 olive eggs. The common eider is a very large duck. The male has a white head and back, black crown and belly. The female is a rich brown with many bars or stripes. *Range:* Coasts of Alaska and Canada; winters to northern Pacific and northern Atlantic coasts.

Harlequin *Histrionicus histrionicus* Length: 14.5-21 in. (37-53 cm)
These birds spend most of their lives on the ocean, but breed inland. Their diet consists of insects, crustaceans, and mollusks. The nest is built in a rock cavity or hollow stump and holds 6-8 buff-colored eggs. The male is gray-blue with a black crown, reddish-brown sides, and is marked with white patches. The female is gray brown and has three white patches on the sides of the head. *Range:* Central Alaska and northwest Canada to central California and Colorado; also eastern coast of Canada. Winters south along coasts to California and to Florida.

surf scoter

white-winged scoter

oldsquaw

common eider

harlequin

MERGANSERS (Subfamily: Merginae)

These fish-eating diving ducks have a long thin bill which is serrated on the sides and well suited for holding live fish. These large but streamlined water birds dive and swim quickly, and have smaller wings which do not interfere with diving.

Hooded Merganser *Lophodytes cucullatus* Length: 16-19 in. (41-48 cm)

This duck is uncommon and the smallest of the mergansers. They dive on ponds or streams for insects and small fish, tadpoles, crustaceans. They build the nest in a tree cavity and lay 6-18 glossy-white round eggs. Both sexes have a white speculum. The male has a black-bordered white crest on top of the head, a black face and neck, white breast with two black bars in front of each wing, brown sides. The female is brownish gray with a white breast and has bushy buff-colored sides. *Range:* Southeast Alaska, Canada, and northern United States; winters to northern Mexico and to Gulf of Mexico.

Red-breasted Merganser *Mergus serrator* Length: 19.5-26 in. (50-66 cm)

This duck spends much of its life in salt water around river mouths, in channels of salt water marshes, or off shore. The nest is built on the ground protected under a log or dwarf evergreen near salt water; 8-10 olive-tan eggs are laid. Both sexes are crested and have white speculums. The male has a green and black head, black back, rusty-red breast, and white collar. The female is gray and has a reddish head—similar in appearance to the common merganser but lacking contrast between the head and the throat. *Range:* Alaska and Canada; winters along Pacific coast to Baja California and eastern U.S. from Great Lakes south to Texas and Florida.

Common Merganser *Mergus merganser* Length: 22-27 in. (56-69 cm)

This is a common species, primarily a fresh water bird, but occasionally they can be seen on brackish waters of bays and inlets. The nesting area is always located close to a brook or a lake; 9-12 buff-colored eggs are laid. Both sexes have a pinkish breast and white wing patch. The male has a greenish-black head, black back, but seldom shows a crest—unlike the female and other mergansers. The female is gray with a red-brown crest on the head and has a white throat. *Range:* Southern Alaska, southern half of Canada, northern part of U.S. from Pacific Coast to Great Lakes; winters to Mexico, Texas, and Florida.

Duck

hooded merganser

red-breasted merganser

common merganser

EAGLES   (Order: Falconiformes, Family: Accipitridae, Subfamily: Buteoninae)

Bald Eagle   *Haliaeetus leucocephalus*   Length: 30-43 in. (75-108 cm)
Eagles are flesh eaters, the primary diet consisting of fish. They may catch the fish themselves or steal it from ospreys. Eagles also catch injured waterfowl, muskrats, squirrels, rabbits and other animals killed by road traffic. The order is characterized by a heavy, sharp, hooked bill, and toes with strong, curved talons. The sexes are alike, but the female is larger than the male. The bald eagle is rare and found locally along shores. The nest is built high in trees or cliffs, and will contain 1-5 dull white eggs. The adult bird has a white head and short white tail on brown body, and a massive yellow bill, which is nearly as long as the head. For the first four years, immature birds are brown with irregular white mottling; the bill is brown. Wingspread is 7-8 feet. *Range:* Alaska and Canada to southern United States.

OSPREYS   (Order: Falconiformes, Family: Pandionidae)

Osprey   *Pandion haliaetus*   Length: 21-24.5 in. (53-61 cm)
Worldwide, this is the only member of its family, but it is one of the most widely distributed birds in the world. They are uncommon, found along seacoasts, bays and unfrozen lakes and rivers. Ospreys are birds of prey which hover, then plunge feet-first for fish, which they eat almost exclusively, only rarely feeding on small rodents and birds. The "fish hawk" builds a sturdy nest of sticks on a treetop or ledge; 4-6 eggs are laid. Sexes are alike, but females are larger than males. The head is primarily white, but with broad dark cheek patch. Plumage is dark above, white below; black "wrist" mark around each leg. *Range:* Worldwide distribution.

HERONS, BITTERNS and **EGRETS** (Order: Ciconiformes, Family: Ardeidae)
These are wading birds with long legs, neck and long straight bill. They fly slowly with th head drawn back, neck folded in an S. Egrets are actually herons but were given th name because of the long plumes "aigrettes" they bear during the breeding season. Bitterns differ by having shorter legs, and a shorter, heavier body. Food consists of fish, frogs and other aquatic life; insects, mice. Sexes are similar.

Great White Heron   *Ardea herodias*   Length: 42-52 in. (107-130 cm)
This magnificent bird is now generally considered to be a south Florida color morph and subspecies of the great blue heron, rather than a separate species, *Ardea occidentalis*, as it was classifed. It is the largest of the white herons. It interbreeds freely with the great blue heron. The heron is white overall with yellow legs and bill. The yellowish legs distinguish it positively from the common egret which has blackish legs. *Range:* Along salt water coast in southern Florida and the Florida Keys, Cuba, Isle of Pines, coast of Yucatan.

bald eagle

osprey

great white heron

Green Heron *Butorides virescens* Length: 16-22 in. (40-55 cm)
This is the most widely distributed of the herons, found in both fresh and salt water. From a distance, the greenish back feathers of this crow-size bird appear blue. The nest is built of sticks high in a tree, or sometimes on the ground. Male and female both incubate the 4-5 greenish-blue eggs. Sexes alike. It has a chestnut colored neck, white chin and throat stripe; back is grayish green; wings are greenish; dark underparts. The legs are yellowish or orange. *Range:* Northwest United States and southeast Canada to northern South America.

Great Blue Heron *Ardea herodias* Length: 42-52 in. (107-130 cm)
This large heron is common on both fresh and salt water. Food preference is fish, but they eat frogs, snakes, crustaceans, birds, small mammals, insects. Nests are built in treetops, shrubs or on the ground; 3-7 greenish-blue eggs are laid. The head is mostly white with black crown patches and head plumes, undersides are dark, back is bluish gray. Young birds have black crown and lack the head plumes. *Range:* Southern Alaska and Canada to Mexico; winters to northern South America.

Reddish Egret *Dichromanassa rufescens* Length: 27-32 in. (69-81 cm)
This uncommon heron is found on saltwater flats. Eats small fishes, frogs, tadpoles, crustaceans which it stirs up from the bottom while wading. The nest is made of twigs and stems and contains 3-4 bluish-green eggs which are incubated by both parents. The head and neck are shaggy and chestnut colored; body is gray, legs are dark. The bill is flesh colored and has a black tip—important in identifying the rare white phase of this bird. *Range:* Baja California, coast of Texas, southern Florida, south to West Indies; winters south to Venezuela.

Little Blue Heron *Florida caerulea* Length: 20-29 in. (51-74 cm)
This is a common heron that is found in both fresh and salt water. But it is primarily an inland bird and prefers freshwater ponds, marshes, lakes. Skilled at fishing, but it prefers to eat crustaceans, frogs and insects. Their delicate nest is made of twigs in bushes contains 4-5 bluish-green eggs. They have a black-tipped bill, reddish-brown head and neck, gray-blue body and dark legs. Young are white with a dark-tipped bluish bill, greenish legs. *Range:* Eastern United States south to Peru, Argentina. Some reports of sightings in California.

Louisiana Heron *Hydranassa tricolor* Length: 26 in. (65 cm)
One of the most abundant herons in the south, this bird breeds on islands off Texas, in Louisiana tidal marshes and on the mangrove and buttonwood islands in Florida. The stick nest is built in a tree or on the ground in grass or weeds; 3-4 bluish-green eggs are laid and incubated by both parents. It eats fishes of no commercial value, amphibians, crayfishes, snails, worms and insects. This is a dark heron with a white belly and rump. The neck appears particularly slender. Young have reddish neck and head, brownish green back. *Range:* Baja California, Atlantic coast from Maryland south around to Gulf Coast; south to northern South America.

green heron

great blue heron

reddish egret

little blue heron

Louisiana heron

Black-crowned Night Heron *Nycticorax nycticorax* Length: 23-28 in. (58-70 cm)
This bird is stocky, thick billed and short legged, usually seen in its hunched inactive stance during the day; it is largely, but not strictly, nocturnal. It is common in fresh-water swamps and tidal marshes. Small fishes are its main food, but it also eats algae and succulent plants. The nest is made of sticks and weeds; the 3-5 bluish-green eggs are incubated by both parents. Back is blackish, black cap on head; underparts are pale gray or whitish; gray wings. Eyes are red, legs are yellowish or yellow-green. During breeding legs are pink and there are two long white plumes on the head. Immature bird is brown, spotted and streaked with white. Sexes alike but males are larger. *Range:* Southern Canada to Argentina.

Yellow-crowned Night Heron *Nyctanassa violacea* Length: 22-28 in. (55-70 cm)
This night heron stalks prey at night, but frequently can be seen feeding during the day. Unlike other herons, this bird rarely eats fish, but feeds mostly on crayfishes and some crabs; also eats frogs, insects, small reptiles, snails, terrapins. The bulky stick nest holds 3-5 blue-green eggs. The chunky, gray adult has a distinct black face with whitish cheek patch and crown. Head plumes are white, long legs are orange yellow. The young are similar to the young of the black-crowned but are duskier with smaller light spots; have shorter, thicker bill; longer legs. *Range:* Oklahoma to Ohio, Atlantic coast from Massachusetts south to Brazil.

American Bittern *Botaurus lentiginosus* 24-34 in. (61-86 cm)
This stocky brown heron is rather common but elusive in tall vegetation of fresh- or salt-water marshes. Sometimes it can be seen frozen in position with head pointed upward in an attempt to hide. The American bittern is most active at dusk and at night. Favorite foods include frogs, small eels, fishes; also eats snakes, salamanders, crayfishes, mice, insects. The nest is built on a platform of dead cattails or bulrushes and holds 4-6 buff colored eggs. The bird has brown upperparts, white throat, long neck with black stripe on each side; in flight the blackish flight feathers are characteristic. *Range:* Marshlands of the United States and Canada; winters to Central America.

Snowy Egret *Egretta thula* Length: 20-27 in. (50-68 cm)
This rather small white heron is common, found primarily in fresh- and salt-water marshes, and sometimes in ponds. Feeds on fishes, frogs, salamanders, water moccasins, crayfishes, rats, aquatic insects. The nest is a frail platform of sticks built in a bush or small tree; 4-5 bluish-green eggs are laid. Both sexes incubate the eggs. The body and plumes are white, with the back plumes curving upward during breeding; black legs and slender black bill; feet are yellow. Immature birds have yellow stripe on the back of the legs. *Range:* California and Idaho to Oklahoma, the Gulf Coast, New Jersey, south to southern South America.

Common Egret *Casmerodius albus* Length: 37-41 in. (94-104 cm)
This large, slender white heron is common along streams, ponds, mudflats, and fresh- and salt-water marshes, where it feeds on fishes, reptiles, amphibians, crayfishes, mice, insects. The nest is built from sticks and stems in a treetop or in bulrushes above water; 3-4 blue-green eggs are laid. Plummage is white, bill is yellow, legs and feet are black; long white plumes on breeding birds. *Range:* United States to southern South America.

Cattle Egret *Bubulcus ibis* Length: 20 in. (50 cm)
A very common heron which can be seen in flocks feeding on insects in dry or moist pastures. Nest made of twigs in swamp trees holds 3-5 blue eggs. White body, but when breeding has buffy orange breast, crest, and back plumes. Bill is yellow or orange and feet are yellowish to pinkish. *Range:* Along coasts from Ontario to Florida and Texas, south to West Indies and South America. Spreading steadily.

Herons, Bittern, Egrets

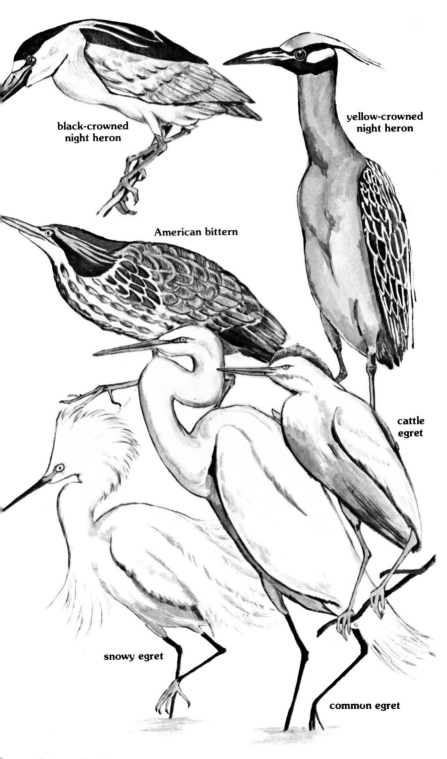

black-crowned
night heron

yellow-crowned
night heron

American bittern

cattle
egret

snowy egret

common egret

Least Bittern *Ixobrychus exilis* Length: 11-14 in. (28-35 cm)
This is the smallest member of the heron family. It prefers to run or climb rather than fly since it is a poor flyer. It feeds at the edge of the water, head darting out after fishes amphibians, crayfishes, slugs, mice, insects. The nest is a platform built on stalks above shallow water; it holds 4-5 bluish or greenish eggs. The neck is chestnut colored, there is a large buff wing patch, two whitish stipes on back. Underparts are brown or buff with dark side patch. The male's head and back is greenish black; female's head and back is purplish-brown, throat is streaked. *Range:* Southeast Canada and United States south to South America.

STORKS (Order: Ciconiiformes, Family: Ciconiidae)

Wood Stork (Wood Ibis) *Mycteria americana* Length: 34-47 in. (85-118 cm)
This long-legged wading bird is the only American stork. The bill is long and thick and decurved. They fly with head and neck extended forward and legs trailing behind. It is locally common in southern swamps, marshes and ponds. They feed on fish, frogs tadpoles, snakes, young alligators and other aquatic animals including insects. The nest is a flimsy platform of sticks built in the swamp in giant cypress trees or in mangroves; 3-dull white eggs are laid. Both parents incubate the eggs. The dark gray head is featherless; neck is gray; greenish-black flight feathers and tail; white body. Male is larger than female. Immature birds have a feathered head and dingy white body. *Range:* Florida and coastal area of Mexico, Central and South America. Spotty in southwest United States.

IBISES and SPOONBILLS (Order: Ciconiiformes, Family: Threskiornithidae)

These are long-necked, long-legged wading birds that fly with their head and neck extended forward and the legs dangling behind. The ibises are heron-like wading birds with a slender, decurved bill. Spoonbills have spatulate bills. They feed on small fish and crustaceans, insects. Sexes are alike.

Roseate Spoonbill *Ajaia ajaja* Length: 32 in. (80 cm)
These are rare birds, found in shallow salt water in their localities. The bill is flattened at the tip. When feeding, the partly opened bill is swung from side to side in mud and water feeling for small fishes, crustaceans, mollusks which they then trap by snapping the bill shut. The nest is made of sticks and twigs in dense low tree or bush and holds 2-3 white brown-spotted eggs. Adults are bright pink with darked pink area on wings. Head is featherless, greenish gray; neck is white. Immature birds are whitish turning pinker with age. *Range:* Gulf states to Chile and Argentina.

White Ibis *Eudocimus albus* Length: 22-27 in. (55-68 cm)
These birds are locally abundant along the coast. When feeding it probes the mud with the slender bill, searching for crustaceans, fishes, small snakes and other water animals and insects. The twig nest is built in low trees or bushes over water; 3-4 greenish-white eggs with brown speckles are laid. Both parents incubate the eggs. The body is white black on wing tips; red on face, legs and long bill. Young birds have gray head and neck brown back, white underparts. *Range:* Coastal areas from Baja California to South Carolina; south to northern South America; West Indies.

FLAMINGO (Order: Ciconiiformes: Family: Phoenicopteridae)

American Flamingo *Phoenicopterus ruber* Length: 45 in. (113 cm)
These wading birds have extremely long legs and neck. The bill is thick and bent sharply down. They eat small mollusks, crustaceans, algae while the bill or head is under water These birds nest in colonies from hundreds to thousands of pairs, on mud flats or mar The cone shaped nest contains 1, rarely 2, chalk white egg. The plummage varies from light pink to rose. *Range:* Occasional on salt flats of Florida coast; West Indies; Yucatan

Bittern, Stork, Ibis, Spoonbill, Flamingo

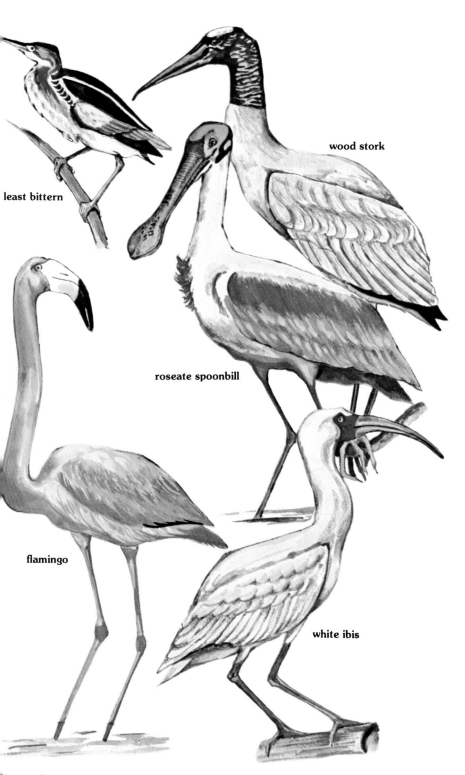

least bittern

wood stork

roseate spoonbill

flamingo

white ibis

Bittern, Stork, Ibis, Spoonbill, Flamingo

CRANES (Order: Gruiformes, Family: Gruidae)

Sandhill Crane *Grus canadensis* Length: 40-48 in. (100-120 cm)
This crane is common in prairies and fields within its locale. They feed on small rodents frogs, and insects. The nest, which is a mound of plants and grasses, may be 4-5 f across. It is built in shallow pond water or on the ground in marshes; it holds 1-3 brow spotted olive eggs which are incubated by both parents. Adults are gray with a bald re crown and bustle-like rear. Immature bird is brown. *Range:* Northern Alaska an Canada south to California, Wyoming, Minnesota, Michigan; also Mississippi an Georgia south to Cuba; winters to Mexico.

LIMPKINS (Order: Gruiformes; Family: Aramidae)

Limpkin *Aramus guarauna* Length: 28 in. (70 cm)
The only New World representative of the family, the limpkin is a large wading bird whic is locally common in marshes, swamps. It feeds primarily on snails, but also eats lizards frogs, insects, worms, crayfish. The nest is a platform of dry rushes built just above wate in saw grass, shrubs; 4-8 buff eggs are incubated by both parents. The limpkin has lon legs and a long slender, slightly decurved bill. The spotted bird is brown; each feather ha a large white crescent. Sexes are alike. *Range:* Southeast United States, West Indies Mexico south to Argentina.

GALLINULES, COOTS, and **RAILS** (Order: Gruiformes, Family: Rallidae)
These are wading birds with long legs. Gallinules and coots swim and resemble duck except for having smaller heads and chicken-like bills. Rails are compact, hen-shape marsh birds. They feed on aquatic plants, seeds, buds, insects, frogs, crustaceans mollusks. Sexes in this family are alike.

Purple Gallinule *Porphyrula martinica* Length: 13 in. (33 cm)
This very colorful bird swims, wades, and climbs bushes. It feeds in rice fields eating grai and seeds; in the marsh it eats frogs, snails, aquatic insects, worms and occasionally egg and young of other small marsh birds. The grass nest is suspended among and wove into surrounding marsh plants; there are 5-10 pink-buff eggs which are spotted wit brown. The red bill has a yellow tip; the shield on forehead is pale blue; purplish head an underparts, olive upper parts. The legs are yellow and there is white under the tail *Range:* Southeastern United States to Argentina; West Indies; has wandered north t southeast Canada.

Common Gallinule *Gallinula chloropus* Length: 13 in. (33 cm)
Common, this bird can be found in both fresh and salt water. It swims and dives fo seeds, grasses, soft parts of water plants; also feeds on land or walks on floating plants i search of food; it will also eat snails, grasshoppers and other insects. The nest is a mass o dead water plants usually built over water and may be partially floating; 7-12 cinnamon t olive-buff spotted with brown eggs are laid. The bill is tipped in yellow and it has a brigh red frontal plate on the head. The head and underparts are gray; back is brown; whit under tail. *Range:* Southern Canada, United States south to Mexico, South America West Indies.

American Coot *Fulica americana* Length: 13-16 in. (33-40 cm)
This common bird is found on ponds, lakes, marshes, and in salt bays in winter. The nes is made of marsh plants and floats on water attached to reeds or other plants; the 8-1 pink to dark buff eggs are spotted with brown. The body is slate colored with darker hea and neck; brown on back; white bill and white under tail and on trailing edge of wings *Range:* Canada to Baja California and southern Florida; south to Central America Cuba, Ecuador, West Indies.

sandhill crane

limpkin

purple gallinule

common gallinule

American coot

Crane, Limpkin, Gallinules, Coot

Sora *Porzana carolina*   Length: 8-10 in. (20-25 cm)
This common but seldom seen rail is found in densely vegetated marshes. Their die
consists of small mollusks and aquatic insects of the marshes, but can be primarily seec
in summer. The nest is made of cattail leaves and is anchored to plants a few inche
above the water and contains as many as 18 buffy, brown-spotted eggs. Both parent
incubate the eggs. The sora has a yellow bill and black face; breast and cheeks are gray
brownish upperparts, barred flanks, white spots on back and breast. The immature bir
lacks the black face and is buffy brown. *Range:* Canada; western, north central an
northeast United States. Winters from southern U.S. to Peru.

Yellow Rail *Coturnicops noveboracensis*   Length: 7 in. (18 cm)
The yellow rail is rare, small and extremely shy. It is found in fresh and salt marshes, an
in wet meadows and grainfields. Its food is limited to small snails, insects, seeds, grasses
cloverleaves. The grass nest contains 8-10 buff, brown-speckled eggs. It has a yellow bil
is yellowish with dark stripes on the back, underparts buff. In flight, a white wing patch i
visible. *Range:* Canada and United States; winters in Oregon, California, souther
Louisiana to southern Florida.

Black Rail *Laterallus jamaicensis*   Length: 5-6 in.(13-15 cm)
This is the smallest of the rails and is locally common in salt marshes. Little is know
about its feeding habits, but it is reported to eat insects, seeds of aquatic plants, and sma
marine crustaceans. The nest is built in the marsh grasses with a roof that conceals 6-1
pink-white eggs with brown spots. It has a black bill and blackish body with white spot
on back. It has red eyes and sepia on the nape of the neck. *Range:* Coast of Californi
locally from Kansas to Massachusetts south along Atlantic coast to central Florid
winters to southern Louisiana and southern Florida, Cuba, West Indies, South Americ

Clapper Rail *Rallus longirostris*   Length: 14-16 in. (35-40 cm)
An abundant occupant of the coastal salt marshes, it is preyed on by hawks, minks
raccoons, turtles, snakes and even big fish. It searches mud flats at low tide for crabs
crayfishes, mollusks, small fishes, aquatic insects and amphibians. The nest is made c
grass and reeds in the marsh and holds 6-14 buff eggs which are blotched with browr
This rather large rail has a long bill, grayish-brown upperparts, white chin, brownis
breast, barred grayish flanks, and a white patch under the short tail. *Range:* Along th
coasts from California to Peru and Connecticut to Brazil.

King Rail *Rallus elegans*   Length: 15-19 in. (38-48 cm)
This large common rail is found in freshwater marshes and occasionally in brackis
marshes. It eats crustaceans, small fishes, frogs, insects, seeds; in winter it also eat
grains and berries. The cup-shaped nest is made of leaves and stalks and is hidden i
clumps of cattails. The 6-15 buff eggs are spotted with brown and are incubated by bot
parents. The king rail has a long beak, streaked rusty brown upperparts, white chin
barred gray flanks, and white patch under the short tail. *Range:* Eastern Nebraska an
central Minnesota to Massachusetts, south to Texas, Florida, Cuba; winters to souther
Mexico.

sora

yellow rail

black rail

clapper rail

king rail

OYSTERCATCHERS (Order: Charadriiformes; Family: Haematopodidae)
These large shorebirds are waders with long laterally flattened red bills which are used to pry shellfish from rocks and open them. They feed on mollusks, crabs and marine worms. Sexes are alike.

American Oystercatcher *Haematopus palliatus* Length: 17-21 in. (43-53 cm)
This noisy bird is not common. It is usually seen on coastal mudflats and sandy beaches in small flocks separated from other shorebirds. It feeds primarily on bivalves, but will also eat small sea urchins, starfish, crabs, marine worms. The nest is a shallow depression in the sand and holds 2-3 spotted green-brown or buffy eggs. They have a black head and neck, long red bill, brownish back, flesh colored legs; wing patches, rump and underparts are white. Female is larger than the male. *Range:* Coasts from Massachusetts to Florida, Texas, Mexico, West Indies, Argentina; Baja California to Chile.

Black Oystercatcher *Haematopus bachmani* Length: 15-17.5 in. (38-44 cm)
This uncommon bird prefers rocky shorelines. It eats mussels, marine worms, but primarily limpets which are plentiful on surf-hammered rocks. The nest is a hollow in beach gravel or in a rocky islet or reef; 2-3 spotted buffy eggs are laid and are incubated by both parents. The head and underparts are black, back is dark brown; bill is long and red. *Range:* Coasts from Aleutian Islands to Baja California.

AVOCETS and **STILTS** (Order: Charadriiformes; Family: Recurvirostridae)
These are slim wading birds with extremely long legs and long slender bills. Their diet consists of insects and small marine invertebrates. Sexes are alike.

American Avocet *Recurvirostra americana* 16-20 in. (40-50 cm)
This fairly common bird breeds on shores of marshes and lakes. It eats insects and their larvae, crustaceans, and seeds of aquatic plants. The nest is built on the ground partially concealed by plant life and holds 4 olive eggs which are spotted with brown. The long bill is curved upward. The cinnamon-buff head, neck and breast are gray in winter. Long legs are gray; back and belly are white; black outer wing and diagonal stripe on inner wing. *Range:* Southwest Canada and western United States; winters from southern U.S. to Guatemala.

Black-necked Stilt *Himantopus mexicanus* 13-17 in. (33-43 cm)
The stilt is common, found in fresh- or salt-water beaches, flats, lakes and ponds. The long thin bill is straight. It eats insects and their larvae, crustaceans, some tiny fishes, and seeds of aquatic plants. The nest is on the ground, sometimes in a depression, in the open or partially hidden by plants; there are usually 4 yellow or buff eggs, irregularly spotted with black or brown. The long legs are pink or red; red eyes, black upperparts, underparts, face and eye spot are white. *Range:* West and south east United States to Peru.

American oystercatcher

American avocet

black oystercatcher

black-necked stilt

Oystercatchers, Avocet, Stilt

PLOVERS (Order: Charadriiformes; Family: Charadriidae)
These shorebirds are small to medium sized and have a shorter neck and bill than sandpipers. The dove-like head is usually strongly marked. They eat small marine life, mealworms. Sexes are similar.

Mountain Plover *Charadrius montanus* Length: 8-9 in. (20-23 cm)
Strangely, this is a shorebird that lives primarily away from water in the high plains and semi-desert regions of the West. Its primary diet consists of insects. The nest is a slight depression on the open ground and holds 2-4 olive eggs spotted and scrawled with black. There is a black patch on the crown and black eye stripe on grayish brown upperparts; underparts are white. Black markings are absent in winter. *Range:* Montana and Kansas south to Mexico and Texas; winters to Baja California and Mexico; accidental in Florida and Massachusetts.

Black-bellied Plover *Pluvialis squatarola* Length: 10.5-13.5 in. (26-34 cm)
This large plover is common. Along the seacoasts they feed on small marine life; on inland shores of lakes they eat insects, seeds, berries. The nest is a hollow in tundra moss and holds 4 eggs which may be gray, green, whitish or brown and spotted overall with brown and black. Breeding birds have a black breast and pale speckled back; black bill and face; rump and tail are white. Young and winter birds are grayish and have a black underwing patch. *Range:* Circumpolar arctic; winters along both U.S. coasts to central S.A.

American Golden Plover *Pluvialis dominica* Length: 9-11 in. (23-28 cm)
The lesser golden plover, as it is also called, is common on the arctic tundra where it nests. The nest is a moss lined depression containing 3-4 eggs which are cinnamon to light buff, heavily marked with black and brown. It eats insects, small mollusks and crustaceans. Breeding birds are dark with golden spots above; underparts black. There is a broad white stripe over the eye and down the side of the neck and breast. Winter adults and young are brown overall, the underside being lighter in hue. *Range:* Arctic; winters in South America, Hawaii; during migration on coast from N.J. to Va.

Piping Plover *Charadrius melodus* Length: 6.5-7.5 in. (15-19 cm)
An uncommon plover, it is the color of the drier sands of beaches that it frequents. It eats insects and other small marine animals and their eggs. The nest is a hollow in the sand above the high water line; 3-4 eggs, gray to pale sand color lightly spotted with purple and black. The bill is black and yellow, they have a black forehead and neck ring. Upperparts are pale ash, underparts are white; legs are yellow orange. In winter the black markings are less distinguishable. *Range:* Southern Canada to central and northeast U.S.; winters along Gulf and Atlantic coast from Texas to South Carolina.

Wilson's Plover *Charadrius wilsonia* Length: 7-8 in. (18-20 cm)
Uncommon and a local bird, it inhabits sandy beaches and mudflats, where it feeds on crabs, small marine life, insects and insect larvae. The nest is scraped out of the sand, sometimes in loose colonies, but more often alone; 3-4 buffy eggs are covered with black and brown markings. They have a thick black bill; upperparts are sandy, underparts are white; legs are pinkish. Male has black patch on crown and eyes, black collar; black markings are absent in female and young, and in the winter male. *Range:* Coasts from Texas to Virginia; winters to Brazil.

Semipalmated Plover *Charadrius semipalmatus* Length: 6.5-7.5 in. (16-19 cm)
This small, plump plover frequents the shores and tideflats. On the shores it eats small marine animals and eggs, insects and larvae; inland it eats great numbers of grasshoppers. They nest in loose colonies in depressions in sand or gravel; 3-4 buffy eggs are boldly marked with black and brown. The bill is black and orange; there is a black bar on the crown and black band on the breast. Upperparts are gray-brown, underparts are white; legs are orange yellow. In winter, bill is black and chest band fades to brownish color. *Range:* Arctic Alaska and Canada; winters along coasts to S.A., West Indies.

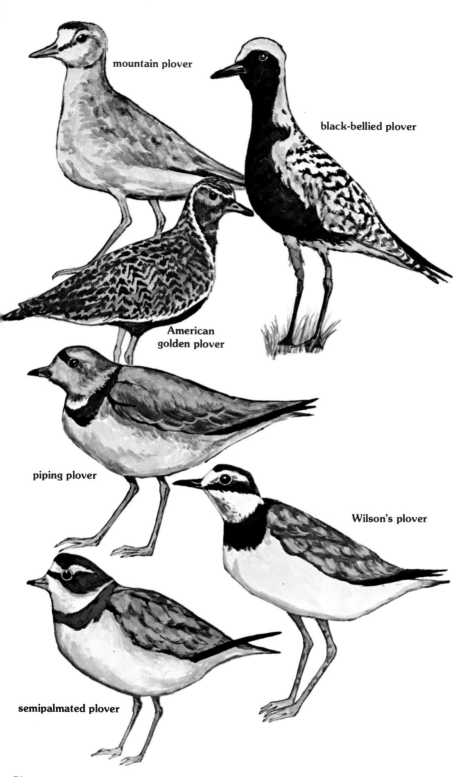

mountain plover

black-bellied plover

American
golden plover

piping plover

Wilson's plover

semipalmated plover

Plovers

SANDPIPERS (Order: Charadriiformes; Family: Scolopacidae)

This is a large and varied group of wading and shore birds which are primarily found along ocean shores, but some are found upland and around fresh water. Their legs and bills are long and slender, and in some species the bills are curved. They feed primarily on small invertebrates. Outside of the breeding season, sandpipers are generally found in flocks. Sexes are alike or similar.

Spotted Sandpiper *Actitis macularia* Length: 7-8 in. (18-20 cm)

This very common sandpiper is found on saltwater coasts in winter and along fresh water during the breeding season. Along the shores it can be seen feeding on small marine invertebrates, but, inland, will also eat all kinds of insects. The nest is a grass-lined depression on the ground, usually hidden by grasses; 4 eggs are green buff to pink buff, spotted with brown. Upperparts are olive brown, underparts are white with round black spots; white wing stripe and white line over the eye. Winter birds lack the black spots on the underparts. *Range:* Alaska and Canada to central U.S.; winters along U.S. coasts to West Indies, Central America and to central South America.

Solitary Sandpiper *Tringa solitaria* Length: 8-9 in. (20-23 cm)

Another common sandpiper, it is often seen with the spotted sandpiper along streams, lakes, swamps. As the common name implies, it is usually seen alone, but also in pairs and in small groups. It eats insects, small crustaceans and frogs. The solitary sandpiper nests in trees in the abandoned nests of blackbirds and other birds; 4 eggs are green or cream buff marked with brown, violet. Black upperparts have light speckles; whitish breast has dark speckles. There is a white eye ring, white belly, barred white tail, long dark legs. Young birds are lighter in color. *Range:* Alaska and Canada; winters from Gulf of Mexico and south Georgia to Argentina.

Long-billed Curlew *Numenius americanus* Length: 20-26 in. (50-65 cm)

This rather common curlew is found in high plains, rangeland, farms, tideflats, beaches and salt marshes. On coasts and shores it eats invertebrates, toads; on land eats insects and at times, berries. The nest is a grass- or weed-lined hollow in moist meadows or dry prairies; 4 eggs are white to buff or deep olive, spotted overall with dark brown. Buff upperparts are mottled, underparts are streaked; cinnamon wing linings. It has a very long (4.5-8.75 in.) downcurved bill. *Range:* Southwest Canada and western U.S.; winters southern U.S. to Guatemala and northern Gulf coast and southeast Atlantic coast.

Whimbrel *Numenius phaeopus* Length: 15-19 in. (38-48 cm)

The whimbrel has a long downcurved bill, but it is shorter than the long-billed curlew's. It feeds on small invertebrates and will eat wild berries. The nest is a saucer-shaped depression in mosses or grasses on the tundra; 3-5 olive eggs are spotted with brown. It has a long curved bill and stripe across the crown; upperparts are mottled grayish brown; whitish underparts are streaked with brown. *Range:* Arctic Alaska and Canada; winters along coasts from central California to southern Chile and north Gulf Coast and southeast Atlantic to South America.

Marbled Godwit *Limosa fedoa* Length: 16-20 in. (40-50 cm)

The marbled godwit can be recognized by its call, *god-wit*. On shores it preys on mollusks, crustaceans and worms; on prairies it eats grasshoppers and other insects, also tubers and seeds. The nest is a hollow in grass on grassy prairies close to water; 4 olive-brown eggs are lightly spotted with brown. This godwit has a long, slightly upturned bill. Upperparts are mottled buffy brown; underparts are brown; cinnamon wing lining. *Range:* Great plains; winters on coasts from central California and South Carolina to Guatemala.

spotted sandpiper

solitary sandpiper

long-billed curlew

whimbrel

marbled godwit

Sandpipers

Long-billed Dowitcher *Limnodromus scolopaceus* Length: 11-12.5 in. (28-31 cm)
This species is larger and has a longer bill (3 in.) than the short-billed dowitcher. They prefer shallow fresh water and soft mud bars where they probe for food. Primary diet is insects, but they will eat marine invertebrates and plant food. The nest is a leaf-lined depression in grass or moss in a marsh; 4 brown to olive eggs are marked with brown and gray. The neck, breast and sides are speckled reddish brown; mottled back is dark; sides are barred. *Range:* Alaska and northwest Canada; winters from central California and Gulf Coast to Guatemala.

Short-billed Dowitcher *Limnodromus griseus* Length: 10.5-12 in. (26-30 cm)
A common bird, found along coastal bays or inland lakes or marshes. Insects are the primary food, but it will eat marine invertebrates, plant food; along coasts it will eat eggs of king or horseshoe crabs. The nest is a hollow in clump of grass at edge of the tundra; 4 buff green or brown eggs are marked with small brown specks. They have a long bill, speckled reddish-brown neck, breast, and sides; dark mottled back; white rump and belly. White rump patch extends up the back. Winter birds have a gray back and breast. *Range:* Alaska and Canada; winters along coast from central California, the Gulf Coast and South Carolina to north South America.

Greater Yellowlegs *Tringa melanoleuca* Length: 14 in. (35 cm)
In summer, this sandpiper is common on the muskeg in Canada and Alaska. It feeds on fish, insects and their larvae, marine invertebrates, tadpoles, berries. The nest is a slight depression on the ground in wet clearings in muskeg country or at edge of tundra; 4 buff eggs are irregularly marked with brown, gray. The upperparts are dark gray; underparts are light, neck and chest speckled; whitish rump and barred whitish tail; legs are bright yellow. *Range:* Alaska and Canada; winters from United States to Tierra del Fuego.

Willet *Catoptrophorus semipalmatus* Length: 14-17 in. (35-43 cm)
This common wading bird is seen in pairs or small flocks. It feeds on aquatic insects, marine invertebrates, small fish, grasses, seeds, rice. The nest is on the ground on offshore islands or coastal beaches, edges of dunes; in west U.S. on open prairies or in short marsh grass. The bird lays 4 olive eggs which are boldly marked with brown. The willet is gray, has black and white wing patches, white tail; legs are bluish. *Range:* Central southern Canada to Gulf of Mexico, West Indies; winters from southern U.S. to Brazil.

Lesser Yellowlegs *Tringa flavipes* Length: 10-11 in. (25-28 cm)
The lesser yellowlegs is a fairly common bird which is smaller and has a shorter and more slender bill than the greater yellowlegs. Primary diet is aquatic insects, but also eats small invertebrates, fish, spiders. The nest is a depression in the ground in grassy marshes and bogs; 4 buff eggs are marked with brown. Upperparts are dark gray; underparts are light; neck and chest are speckled; white rump and barred white tail; bright yellow legs. *Range:* Alaska and Canada; winters from southern United States to Argentina.

Sandpipers

long-billed dowitcher

short-billed dowitcher

greater yellowlegs

willet

lesser yellowlegs

Sandpipers

Ruddy Turnstone *Arenaria interpres* Length: 8-10 in. (20-25 cm)
The slender pointed bill of the turnstone is slightly upturned at the tip. The bill is used to overturn stones while feeding on amphipods, worms, insects and their larvae, small mollusks. The nest is a depression on the tundra beside a niche or clump of plants; the 4 eggs are green-olive, densely marked with black spots. The upperparts are harlequin patterned with black, white, brown and chestnut; breast is black, belly is white, legs are orange. Young birds and winter adults are duller and lack the chestnut color. *Range:* Alaska to Greenland; winters from California, Gulf coast, South Carolina south to Chile and Brazil.

Black Turnstone *Arenaria melanocephala* Length: 9 in. (23 cm)
Unmoving on encrusted reefs, this turnstone can be easily overlooked since it resembles a rock or clump of seaweed. It lives along the coasts at the water's edge where it eats barnacles, slugs, small mollusks and crustaceans and other small marine animals. The nest is a depression hollowed out in dead, flat grass; 4 olive-yellow eggs are spotted or blotched with brown. The upperparts and breast are blackish with white speckling; white spot in front of eye, white belly. Winter birds lack the white speckling. *Range:* Coasts of Alaska; winters to Baja California.

Purple Sandpiper *Calidris maritima* Length: 8-9 in. (20-23 cm)
This darkest east coast sandpiper is common on rocky coasts and jetties. It probes into seaweeds and rock crevices hunting for small crustaceans and mollusks. The nest is a grass-lined hollow on moist or dry tundra near the coast; 4 greenish eggs are marked with sepia and dark lines. Upperparts are slate gray; belly is white; legs are yellow. *Range:* Arctic Canada; winters along coasts from breeding grounds to Florida.

Knot *Calidris canutus* Length: 10-11 in. (25-28 cm)
This stocky bird has a rather short bill and is locally common. It feeds primarily on beaches eating mollusks, crab eggs, small fish, marine worms, seeds and insects. The nest is a hollow in clumps of lichens on high rocky tundra; 4 eggs are buff-olive marked with browns. Washed-out gray upperparts; greenish legs; breast is red in spring, whitish in fall. *Range:* Northern Alaska and arctic Canada; winters from California and Massachusetts to South America.

Western Sandpiper *Calidris mauri* Length: 6-7 in. (15-18 cm)
This sandpiper is common on beaches, shores and mud flats. Feeds primarily on aquatic insects but also eats small crustaceans and mollusks, worms. The nest is a grass-lined depression on moist to dry tundra, sometimes on mossy mountain slopes; 4 cream to light brown eggs are spotted and blotched with sepia. Upperparts are blackish and buff colored with rusty back and crown, chest is speckled, belly is white, legs are black; winter birds lack speckling and have rusty color only on shoulders. *Range:* Coast of Alaska; winters from southern U.S. and Gulf Coast south to Peru.

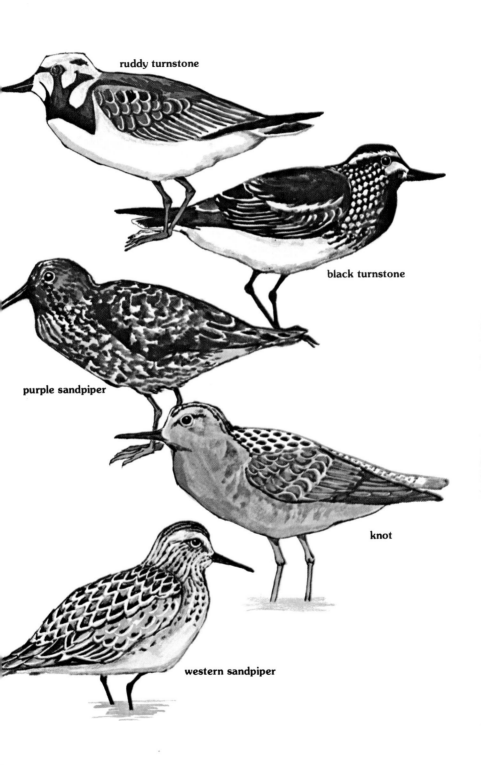

ruddy turnstone

black turnstone

purple sandpiper

knot

western sandpiper

Dunlin *Calidris alpina* Length: 8-9 in. (20-23 cm)
This bird is also known as the red-backed sandpiper, named for the reddish plumage present during breeding season. It feeds on beaches and mud flats on sand fleas and other crustaceans, marine worms, mollusks and insects. The nest is made of grasses or leaves and built on a dry site; 4 green to olive-buff eggs are spotted with gray and reddish brown. Dunlins have a long bill which is curved at the tip. Upperparts are reddish, underparts are light with a black belly patch in spring. Winter birds are brownish gray with a gray chest and white belly. *Range:* Arctic, circumpolar; winters along Pacific, Atlantic and Gulf coasts south to Mexico.

Sanderling *Calidris alba* 7-8 in. (18-20 cm)
This plump, active sandpiper is common on sandy beaches near the edge of the water. It eats tiny crustaceans, mollusks, marine worms on coastal beaches; on nesting islands it eats insects and their larvae. The nest is a depression lined with mosses at the edge or in a patch of low plants; 3-4 dull green-olive or olive-brown eggs are lightly spotted with black and brown. Plumage is rusty above, white below; black wings with bold white wing stripe; legs are black. In winter, birds are pale gray and white. *Range:* Arctic, circumpolar; winters along Pacific, Atlantic and Gulf coasts south to South America.

Semipalmated Sandpiper *Calidris pusilla* 5.5-6.5 in. (14-16 cm)
This is probably the most abundant shore bird, it is found on both fresh and salt water along with western and least sandpipers. It can be differentiated from the least by black legs and grayer body with less markings on the chest, and it has a shorter slimmer bill than the Western. It primarily eats aquatic insects but will eat small mollusks, worms, crustaceans. The nest is a leaf- or grass-lined depression near lakes or grassy coastal dunes; 4 yellow to buff or olive eggs are spotted with warm browns. Upperparts are black and buff, chest is speckled; belly is white, legs are black. Winter birds lack speckling on chest. *Range:* Breeding birds in arctic Alaska and Canada; non-breeding birds found south to Gulf of Mexico and Panama; winters from South Carolina and Gulf of Mexico coasts south through Mexico and West Indies to South America.

Least Sandpiper *Calidris minutilla* Length: 5-6.5 in. (13-16 cm)
This small, very common sandpiper is found on salt marshes and muddy shores of rivers and estuaries. Feeds on insects and insect larvae, worms, small crustaceans and mollusks. The nest is a grass- or leaf-lined cup; 4 buff eggs are randomly marked with dark browns. Upper plumage is streaked brown; white breast is streaked with brown; bill is short and thin; legs are yellow. *Range:* Alaska and Canada; winters from southern U.S. to South America.

Common Snipe *Capella gallinago* Length: 11 in. (28 cm)
This wading bird is found in marshes, bogs and wet meadows. Half of the snipe's diet is made up of insects; it also eats mollusks, crustaceans, worms, lizards, frogs, salamanders. Nest is scraped out of the ground and lined with grass or sedge; 4 dark olive buff or pale olive eggs are irregularly marked with brown. The snipe has a long slender bill, head and upperparts are striped brown and buff; white underparts streaked with brown. In flight, tail shows orange. *Range:* Alaska, Canada and north U.S.; winters south to South America.

American Woodcock *Philohela minor* Length: 11 in. (28 cm)
A rotund nocturnal bird, the American woodcock appears to be neckless. It frequents moist woodlands, swamps and thickets where it feeds primarily on earthworms, but will also eat insects and their larvae. The nest is a leaf-lined depression in the ground in woods; 4 buff or cinnamon eggs are regularly spotted with browns, grays, purple. The eggs are surprisingly large for the size of the bird. The bird is brown with black bars on the back of the head and has a varied black and gray pattern on the back and wings. Bill is long, body is chunky, neck and tail are short; large pop eyes. *Range:* Southeast Canada to Louisiana and Florida; winters in southeast U.S.

dunlin

sanderling

semipalmated
sandpiper

least sandpiper

common snipe

American
woodcock

Sandpipers

PHALAROPES (Order: Charadriiformes; Family: Phalaropididae)
These birds look like sandpipers but they have lobed toes and are swimmers. They are classified by some as members of the sandpiper family *Scolopacidae*. Females are larger and more brightly colored than are the males. They feed on animal marine plankton.

Wilson's Phalarope   *Phalaropus tricolor*   Length: 9 in. (23 cm)
Wilson's phalarope is not pelagic, but is the land dweller in this family. Feeds while walking along muddy shores or wading in shallow water. Eats insect larvae, diving beetles, brine shrimp and aquatic plant seeds. The nest is a grass-lined hollow concealed in grass or marsh; 4 buff eggs are heavily marked with brown spots and splotches. These birds have a long, needle-like bill. Crown is pale, cinnamon neck stripe blending into black eye stripe; back is gray, wings are dark; underparts and rump are white; black legs. Winter birds and young have gray upperparts, white underparts; legs are yellowish or greenish. *Range:* Southwest Canada and western U.S, migratory through plains states and rare in fall along Atlantic coast; winters to South America.

Red Phalarope   *Phalaropus fulicarius*   Length: 8-9 in. (20-23 cm)
This seagoing bird is uncommon, most often sighted in storms along the coast. On land it feeds on mosquitoes, crane flies, aquatic invertebrates; at sea eats fish larvae, small jellyfishes and crustaceans. The nest is a well concealed depression on the tundra near sea or on coastal islands; 4 eggs are gray-buff to olive brown spotted with chestnut and black. In breeding season it has a blackish head, white cheeks and wing stripe; back is striped brown, underparts reddish, legs are yellow. Winter adults and young have grayish upperparts and white underparts and black patch through the eye. *Range:* Arctic coasts from Alaska to Greenland; winters at sea to southern Atlantic and Pacific oceans.

SKUAS and **JAEGERS** (Order: Charadriiformes, Family: Stercorariidae)
These dark hawk-like seabirds have slightly hooked beaks. They harass other smaller seabirds like gulls and terns, forcing them to disgorge fishes they have eaten which is the stercorarids primary source of food. They also eat dead fish and seabirds. On nesting grounds they eat lemmings and other rodents, carrion and small birds. Their long, slender wings are distinctively bent in flight, unlike other seabirds. Sexes are alike.

Skua   *Catharacta skua*   Length: 21-24 in. (53-60 cm)
This strong and swift flyer has a distinctive white wing patch. It is a pirate, harassing other seabirds more than the jaegers. The nest is a depression lined with grass built in colonies on rocky slopes or at the base of a cliff; two yellow to green or brown eggs are marked with browns, purple. The brownish body is lightly streaked with buff; white wing patch, hooked bill, short blunt tail. *Range:* Breeds locally in cold waters of north Atlantic, southern Pacific and Antarctic; wanders widely at sea in Pacific and Atlantic.

Pomarine Jaeger   *Stercorarius pomarinus*   Length: 22 in. (55. cm)
The pomarine is the largest of the jaegers and has a proportionately larger bill. The nest is a slight depression above the tundra; 2-3 brown to green eggs are lightly spotted with browns, grays. Dark phase is sooty gray overall; light phase has sooty head cap, back; sides of neck are yellow, underparts are white. The projecting central tail feathers are broad and twisted. Young lack long tail and are marked with dusky and buffy bars. *Range:* Arctic; winters at sea from southern U.S. to southern hemisphere.

Parasitic Jaeger   *Stercorarius parasiticus*   Length: 18 in. (45 cm)
This is the most common jaeger, often seen pursuing gulls and terns. Besides eating what it can steal from other seabirds, it eats fish and shellfish found cast up on beaches. They nest in colonies in a depression on the ground; two olive or brown eggs are irregularly marked with browns. The projecting tail feathers are short, flat and pointed. The dark phase is soot colored overall. In the light phase the jaeger has a black head cap, yellow on sides of neck, white chest and underparts; upperparts are grayish. *Range:* Arctic; winters from Florida and southern California south to Chile and Argentina.

Wilson's phalarope

red phalarope

skua

Pomarine jaeger

parasitic jaeger

Phalaropes, Skua, Jaegers   53

GULLS (Order: Charadriiformes, Family: Laridae, Subfamily: Larinae)
Gulls are swimming birds which are also skillful flyers with long pointed wings. They have webbed feet and the tail is usually square shaped. They are primarily scavengers and can be seen in flocks of thousands at garbage dumps or fish docks. They also eat fish and other dead animals washed on shore by the tide. When feeding on water, they alight on the water rather than dive. Sexes are alike. Gulls nest in colonies.

Great Black-backed Gull *Larus marinus* 28-31 in. (70-78 cm)
This common gull is becoming more prevalent and widening its range. It and the lesser black-backed gull (*Larus fuscus*, 23 in., 58 cm), are the only black-backed gulls in the east. It will feed on eggs, young and some adult seabirds in addition to the more normal diet. The nest is a grass-lined depression on a high place; 2-3 brown eggs are spotted. It is a rather large white bird with black back; legs are pink. The lesser is smaller with yellow legs and is a casual visitor to Atlantic coast of U.S. The young are brown with paler undersides. *Range:* Coasts of north North Atlantic; winters to the middle Atlantic states.

Western Gull *Larus occidentalis* Length: 24-27 in. (61-69 cm)
This is a small common gull which follows ships to collect refuse and steals from cormorants and pelicans. The nest is built of weeds and grass near beaches; 3 buff-olive eggs are spotted. They are white with a black back and blackish wing tips; red spot on beak. Young are brownish. *Range:* Northern Washington to northwest Mexico.

Herring Gull *Larus argentatus* Length: 23-26 in. (58-65 cm)
This is the "generic seagull", common on coasts and rivers and lakes. It will eat eggs and young of other seabirds. The nest is a slight hollow in the ground; the 2-3 eggs are varied in color. This is a white bird with a gray back, has a red spot on the beak, and white spots on black wing tips; legs and feet are pink; brown streaks on head in winter. Young birds are grayish. *Range:* Alaska and Greenland to northern U.S. states; winters south to Mexico, Panama, Bermuda and West Indies.

Glaucus-winged Gull *Larus glaucescens* Length: 24-27 in. (61-69 cm)
This abundant gull populates dumps and harbors. The nest of dried straw, seaweeds, is built on a rocky ledge or amid plant life; 2-3 olive-buff eggs are marked with browns. It is white with pale gray back, has whitish spots at wing tips; yellow beak with red spot. Immature birds are mottled gray brown. *Range:* Islands in Bering Sea, western coast of Alaska to northwest Washington; winters south to northern Mexico.

Laughing Gull *Larus atricilla* Length: 16-17 in. (40-43 cm)
This common coastal bird will alight on the head of a brown pelican and take fish from its pouch. The nest is built of weeds and grasses on coastal islands, saltwater marshes, or along beaches; 3-4 brown-olive eggs are marked with brown. The bill and head are red, head and wing tips are black; white eye ring and rear wing edge. Neck and underparts are white; back is dark gray. In winter, bill and feet are gray, head is white with grayish markings. Immature birds are brownish with buff chin, white rump and dark tail band. *Range:* Atlantic and Gulf coasts from Nova Scotia to Venezuela; West Indies; southern California to Mexico. Winters to Peru and Brazil.

Bonaparte's Gull *Larus philadelphia* 12-14 in. (30-36 cm)
A petite gull, it is found inland when breeding and on the coast in winter. When inland its diet is primarily insects. The nest is built of sticks and twigs on a branch; 2-3 buff to olive eggs are evenly marked with brown. In summer it has a black head; legs red, small black bill. Winter adults and immature birds have white head with black earspot. *Range:* Alaska and Canada; winters to Gulf coast, Florida and West Indies.

California Gull *Larus californicus* Length: 20-23 in. (50-58 cm)
A common Pacific coast bird, it lives inland in summer and cleans the farm fields of insects and mice. The nest of weeds is built on islands in freshwater lakes and marshes; 3 olive-buff eggs are irregularly marked. This gull is white with gray back, has yellowish green legs; lower mandible of yellow bill has a red and black spot. Immature birds are mottled brown. *Range:* West coast of North America; casual occurrence in Texas, Florida.

great black-backed gull

western gull

glaucus-winged gull

herring gull

laughing gull

Bonaparte's gull

California gull

TERNS (Order: Charadriiformes, Family: Laridae, Subfamily: Sterninae)
These slender birds have forked tails, a pointed bill and long, narrow wings. They div
headfirst from the air for their food, usually small fish, marine life or insects. Unlike th
gulls, they normally do not swim. Most terns are whitish with a black cap, but the blac
on the forehead is white in winter. Sexes are alike.

Common Tern   *Sterna hirundo*   Length: 13-16 in. (33-40 cm)
This is the most common U.S. tern, found on the coast and inland over large lakes. Th
common tern feeds on small fish, crustaceans and insects. They nest in colonies; nest is
hollow in the soil, smoothed by the body and lined with grasses or seaweeds; 2-3 olive o
brown eggs are spotted. It is a white bird with black cap and nape, gray back, forked tai
orange bill has a black tip. Immature birds and winter adults have black only from eye t
eye on back of head. *Range:* Temperate northern hemisphere; winters to souther
hemisphere.

Roseate Tern   *Sterna dougallii*   Length: 14-17 in. (35-43 cm)
The roseate tern is paler above than the common tern. Diet is almost wholly small fishes
which they catch by hovering over and plunging into the water. They nest in colonies o
sandy or pebbly beaches near shore; 1-2 buff to olive-buff eggs are covered with sma
brown dots. The roseate tern is marked like the common tern but the bill is usually black
sometimes with red at the base; rosy tint on breast is seldom visible. *Range:* Coasts c
Atlantic and Pacific oceans.

Least Tern   *Sterna albifrons*   Length: 9 in. (23 cm)
Also known as the little tern, this very small tern is common on sandy beaches. Their siz
and the yellow beak and legs are characteristic of this species. It eats small fishes an
crustaceans, sand eels, shrimp, prawns. Unlike other terns, the least tern does no
require an isolated place to build its nest. The nest is often a scrape in sand on mainlan
beaches above the tide line; 2 buff to pale olive-buff eggs are marked with dark brown.
has a white forehead and underparts, black cap and line through eye, gray back; feet an
bill are yellow. In winter bill is dark and crown is whitish. *Range:* Temperate and tropic
waters off both U.S. coasts, Mexico, Bahamas, Caribbean; winters to Peru and Brazi

Forster's Tern   *Sterna forsteri*   Length: 14-15 in. (35-38 cm)
This is a tern of fresh and salt marshes, rarely seen on coastal beaches. It is very simila
to the common tern and was not identified as a unique species until mid-19th century.
dives into the water for live fishes, but will eat dead fishes and frogs and many insects
The nest is a depression in mud or sand lined with pieces of shells and grasses; 3-4 egg
are brown or olive, irregularly marked with brown. The orange bill has a black tip, ca
and nape are black, back is gray with silver wing tips, underparts are white; tail is forke
and outer edge is white in summer (dark in common tern). *Range:* Western Canada
western U.S., central Atlantic coast to Mexico; winters from southern U.S. t
Guatemala.

common tern

roseate tern

least tern

Forster's tern

Terns

Royal Tern *Sterna maxima* Length: 18-21 in. (45-53 cm)
This is a large tern which is common, but found only on salt water. It feeds on fish, squid, some mollusks and shrimp; it will steal food from pouch of brown pelican. The nest is a depression in the sand built in closely packed colonies; 1-2, or rarely 3-4, white to pale buff or yellow eggs are spotted with dark brown. The bill is orange; forehead, crest and feet are black; back is pale gray. Winter adults and young have white forehead; forehead turns white early during breeding season, which helps distinguish it from the larger, black-crested Caspian tern. *Range:* Coast of southeast U.S., northwest Mexico, West Indies; winters from southern U.S. to Argentina.

Elegant Tern *Sterna elegans* Length: 16-17 in. (41-43 cm)
It resembles the larger royal tern, but the elegant has a longer black crest and slimmer bill. Its diet is wholly fish. The nest is a hollow scraped in sand on undisturbed beaches; single white to pinkish-buff egg is blotched with brown or black. It has a long black crest; long, slender bill is dark orange-yellow. *Range:* Primarily a Mexican bird which visits the California coastline; breeds along Gulf of California and Pacific Coast near San Diego; winters to northern California coast and South America.

Caspian Tern *Sterna caspia* Length: 19-23 in. (48-58 cm)
The Caspian tern has more gull-like mannerisms than the other terns—it alights on water, robs other sea birds and has wider wings than most terns. It resembles the royal tern but has a much redder bill and ranges inland. It feeds on fish, steals from other sea birds, and sometimes eats eggs or young of other terns and gulls. The nest is a grass or seaweed lined scrape on a sandy island or sometimes on floating plants in a marsh; 1-3 pinkish-buff eggs are lightly spotted with brown. It has a thick red bill, black cap, grayish back, black feet. Winter adult has crown streaked to below eyes. *Range:* Canada, Great Lakes; in west, south to Baja California and Wyoming; in east, coasts of Virginia, South Carolina, Louisiana and Texas; winters to south Baja California and to West Indies.

Black Tern *Chlidonias niger* 9-10 in. (23-25 cm)
Normally found on lakes and fresh marshes, the black tern migrates to seacoasts in fall, where it may be distinguished from the least tern by its plain wings (least has black in the wings). Eats primarily insects; when feeding over water on small fishes, crustaceans and other marine animals, it prefers to snatch them from the surface rather than dive. Nest is built in hollow of fallen dead canes or on floating masses of dead plants; 3 olive or buff eggs are densely marked with brown. The head and body are black; back, tail and wings are gray. In winter, adults and immature birds have white head and underparts. *Range:* in its habitat, throughout temperate North America; winters in Central and South America.

Sooty Tern *Sterna fuscata* Length: 15-17 in. (38-43 cm)
This tern also prefers not to dive; it swoops the surface of the water and picks up fishes and squids in its bill. The nests are built in dense colonies in sand or on flat ground; 1-3 white to buff eggs are marked with lavender or red-brown spots. This bird is jet black above, white below; white forehead; bill and feet black. Immature bird has brown-black back with some white speckling and a dirty-white belly. *Range:* Breeds in Dry Tortugas off Florida Keys; pushed northward and along Florida coasts by hurricanes. Widely distributed in pantropical oceans.

royal tern

elegant tern

Caspian tern

sooty tern

black tern

Terns

AUKS (ALCIDS) (Order: Charadriiformes, Family: Alcidae)
These are pelagic birds which come ashore only to breed. They are expert divers and use their wings to swim under water. In air, they fly with a rapid wingbeat. They eat fish, crustaceans, mollusks, algae. Sexes are alike. Immature birds resemble adults.

Rhinoceros Auklet *Cerorhinca monocerata* Length: 14-15.5 in. (36-39 cm)
Seldom seen by day during breeding season, but this auklet is common along the Pacific coast in winter. It fishes silently at sea where it dives for small fishes and crustaceans, but is very noisy on nesting grounds where it barks, growls and shrieks. The nest is a small pile of sticks, grasses and feathers at the end of a burrow constructed by both parents; one white egg may be spotted with gray or lavender. They have a prominent yellowish or orange-brown bill with a little horn at the base which gives it the name "rhinoceros". They also have a white "whisker" on each side of the face and narrow white plume behind each eye. The body is brownish above, white below; grayish throat and breast; legs pale yellow. Winter adults lack horn, and plumes are shorter. Young are brown and lack horn and white plumes. *Range:* Nests on coasts and offshore islands from southeast Alaska to central California; winters off coast south to Baja California.

Common Puffin *Fratercula arctica* Length: 11.5-13.5 in. (29-34 cm)
Also known as the Atlantic puffin, these birds shed the outer layers of the bill in late summer, so winter adults and immature birds have small bills. It catches small fishes, mollusks and crustaceans underwater, using the wings to swim. The nest is in a burrow of loose soil at tops of cliffs or on islands; single white egg (rarely 2) is round and may have brown spots. It has a parrot-like bill which is bright reddish orange at the tip half and blue outlined with a yellow border at the rear half. Upperparts are black, underparts are white; cheeks are white; feet are reddish orange. Winter adult has dark face and bill is not as high; immature bird has small black bill and gray cheeks. *Range:* North Atlantic from Greenland to New England.

Tufted Puffin *Lunda cirrhata* Length: 14.5-15.5 in. (37-39 cm)
This largest puffin is also the most southern in its distribution. It dives and swims underwater to feed primarily on fishes, but it also eats invertebrates. The nest is in a burrow dug in soil on tops of islands or on sandy bluffs; the single egg is dull white or pale blue, marked with lavender and brown. The body is dark overall, face is white; it has a triangular shaped red bill and long backward-curving straw-color plumes in summer. Winter birds lack the plumes. Immature birds have small triangular bills without any red and undersides are dark gray. *Range:* Shores and offshore islands from Alaska to southern California.

SKIMMERS (Order: Charadriiformes, Family: Rynchopidae)

Black Skimmer *Rynchops niger* Length: 16-20 in. (40-50 cm)
This slim, short-legged relative of the gulls has a lower mandible that is longer than the upper. They fly low over the water with the lower jaw in contact with the water searching for small fishes and crustaceans. The nest, in colonies, is a hollow scraped out of sand on the upper beach above the high-water level; 1-5 blue-white or cream-white eggs are heavily marked with brown, purple, gray. Upperparts and cap are black; white forehead and white below. Scissor-like bill is red with black tip; legs and feet are red. Immature bird is mottled brown above. *Range:* Ocean beaches and saltwater bays from Cape Cod to southern South America; winters from southeast coast of U.S. south. In Florida it can also be found on inland lakes.

rhinoceros auklet

tufted puffin

common puffin

black skimmer

Auks, Skimmer

KINGFISHERS (Order: Coraciiformes, Family: Alcedinidae)

These are chunky, compact birds with large heads which are crested in many species. Except during the nesting season, they are usually solitary birds. The New World species are plunging divers, feeding on fishes, amphibians, crustaceans and water insects; otherwise they are not aquatic. Most are brightly colored. Sexes are similar.

Belted Kingfisher   *Megaceryle alcyon*   Length: 11-14 in. (28-36 cm)
This is the most common North American kingfisher. After catching a fish, it returns to its perch where it stuns the fish by hitting it on a limb and then tosses it in the air and swallows it headfirst. It also feeds the same way on tadpoles, crabs, crayfishes, musssels, reptiles, amphibians, insects, young birds, mice and berries. The nest is a long (3-7 ft.) horizontal or tilted slightly upward burrow dug by the pair in sand, clay or gravel bank, near or away from water; 5-8 white eggs. The birds are blue-gray above with a white collar; white below; band of blue-gray across breast; ragged double crest. Female has rusty band across belly. *Range:* Inland and coastal waters from Alaska and Canada to southern U.S.; winters to Central America, Bermuda, West Indies.

Green Kingfisher   *Chloroceryle americana*   Length: 7-8 in. (18-20 cm)
This bird is easily distinguished by the lack of crest, small size and green back. It plunges from a low perch into water for small minnows. The nest is in a horizontal burrow dug in the bank of a stream; 3-6 white eggs. It is dark glossly green above, has a white collar and belly; wings spotted and barred with white. Male has broad chestnut band across chest; female has two bands of green spots across breast. *Range:* Mexico, Central America, South America; rare straggler in fall and winter into southeast Arizona.

belted kingfisher

green kingfisher

Kingfishers

INDEX

Index